Kitchen and Bath Remodeling Guide

RYAN BRAUTOVICH

Copyright © 2014 Ryan Brautovich

All rights reserved. No part of this book may be reproduced or transmitted in any form or by any means, electronic or mechanical, including photocopying, recording, or by any information storage and retrieval system, without the written permission of the Publisher.

Printed in the United States of America

January 2014

ISBN: 978-0-9864404-9-6

"Quality is never an accident; it is always the result of high intention, sincere effort, intelligent direction and skillful execution; it represents the wise choice of many alternatives."

~ William A. Foster

The Construction H.E.L.P. Foundation's Home Construction Audit program makes it easy and painless – through the use of our Home Building System – to understand how to build a home, how to manage your contractor, and how to protect yourself from being taken advantage of and scammed. We demystify the process and remove all of the contractor jargon to give you the building process in easy-to-understand, plain English. The Construction H.E.L.P. Foundation's founder and building expert Ryan Brautovich's exclusive 4-step home building system will ensure you are on the right track – and on budget – every step of the way. For more information about the Construction H.E.L.P Foundation, the Home Construction Audit Program, or any of the educational products, homeowner services, or construction seminars available in your area, please visit **www.HomeConstructionAudit.com**, or **www.ConHelp4U.org**.

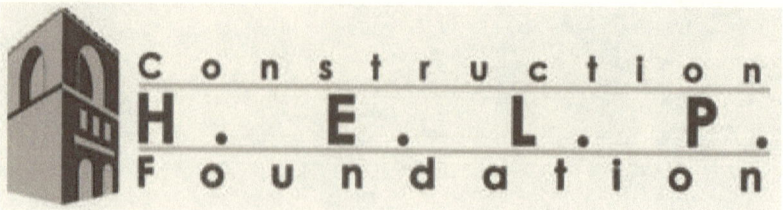

TABLE OF CONTENTS

QUALITY INSPECTION CHECKLIST

CABINETS	1
COUNTER TOPS	3
ELECTRIC (FINAL)	4
FLOOR COVERINGS	5
MIRRORS	7
PAINTING (FINAL)	9
PAINTING (ROUGH)	11
PAINTING (TOUCH-UP)	13
PLUMBING (FINAL)	14
SHOWER DOORS	17
TRIM LABOR	18

COMMON REMODELING CONSTRUCTION DEFECTS

PAINT AND STAIN	20
STAINS FROM UNDERLYING SURFACES BLEED THROUGH	20
PAINT BECOMES CHALKS OR FADES	20
PAINT FLAKING OR PEELING	20
PAINTS APPLED TOO THIN, TOO TICK, OR IN A SPOTTY MANNER	21
PAINT OR STAIN OVERSPRAY ON ADJACENT SURFACES	21
LACQUERS AND VARNISHES PEEL AND FLAKE RAPIDLY	22
STAINED EXTERIOR SURFACES ARE BLOTCHY OR HAVE UNEVEN COLOR	23
PAINTED STUCCO SURFACES DO NOT PERMIT MOISTURE TO ESCAPE	23
BRUSH MARKS OR LAP MARKS SHOW	24
FINISH FLOORING	24
FLOOR NOT LEVEL, FLOOR SQUEAKS, EXCESSIVE DEFLECTION (SAGGING), EXCESSIVE FELEXIBILITY (BOUNCE)	24
HARDWOOD FLOORING	25
CUPPING OR CROWNING OF INDIVIDUAL FLOOR BOARDS	25
SCALLEOPED AND ABRADED SURFACE	25
GAPS BETWEEN ADJACENT FLOOR BOARDS	25

DIFFERENCES IN COLOR BETWEEN INDIVIDUAL FLOOR BOARDS	26
FLOOR BOARDS ON PRE-FINISHED FLOORS ARE NOT LEVEL WITH ONE ANOTHER AT SIDES OR ENDS	26
SPLINTERS OR CHIPS ARE PRESENT AT THE EDGES OF FLOOR BOARDS AFTER INSTALLATION	27
DARK LINES APPEAR PERPENDICULAR TO THE FLOOR BOARD	27
FLOOR BOARDS DISCOLOR AND ROT, PARTICULARLY UNDER AREA RUGS	28
CERAMIC AND CLAY TILE FLOORING	28
CRACKS AND / OR LOOSE TILES	28
GROUT IS CRACKED	28
INDIVIDUAL TILES ARE OUT OF PLANE	29
GRANITE, MARBLE, AND OTHER STONE FLOORING	29
CRACKS	29
STAINS	29
SCRATCHES AND ABRASIONS	30
VINYL FLOORING	30
WIDE SEAMS OR JOINTS	30
DELAMINATION	30
DISCOLORATION	31
ADHESIVE APPEARS ON THE SURFACE THROUGH JOINTS	31
"TELEGRAPHING" OR IRREGULAR SURFACE BEANEATH VINYL FLOORING	32
PATTERN DOES NOT MATCH OR ALIGN	32
CARPET FLOORING	32
VISIBLE SEEMS	32
CARPET IS LOOSE	33
CARPET FIBERS SEPARATE FROM BACKING	33
FADING AND DISCOLORATION	33
CARPET TEXTURE DOES NOT ALIGN AT SEAMS	34
CARPETS HAVE A DARK SOIL LINE AT STAIR AND BASEBOARD EDGES	34
THERE IS A BUMP AT THE TRANSITION BETWEEN CARPET AND HARD SURFACE FLOORING	35
COUNTERTOPS	35
COUNTERTOP IS NOT LEVEL	35
BACKSLASH IS LOOSE	35

CERAMIC TILE COUNTERTOPS	36
UNEVEN SURFACE	36
UNEQUAL GROUT JOINTS	36
GROUT JOINT CRACKS	36
CRACKED TILE	37
COLOR AND TEXTURE VARIATIONS	37
LOOSE TILE	37
WATER PENETRATION THROUGH TOP	38
GRANITE, MARBLE, STONE COUNTERTOPS	38
CRACKS	38
TEXTURE AND COLOR VARIATIONS	39
STAINS	39
CHIPS	39
PLASTIC LAMINATE COUNTERTOPS	40
OPEN JOINTS	40
DELAMINATION	40
UNACCEPTABLE TRIMMING	41
STAINS AND BURNS	41
SOLID SURFACE COUNTERTOPS	41
OPEN SEAMS	41
ROUGHENED SURFACE	42
STAINS AND BURNS	42
BLEMISHES AND SCRATCHES	43
CULTURE MARBLE COUNTERTOPS	43
BLEMISHES AND INCONSISTENT COLOR	43
VOIDS AT SURFACE	44
LEAKS AT JOINTS AND FITTINGS	44
APPLIANCES	44
APPLIANCES DO NOT PERFORM AS INTENDED	44
CABINETS AND VANITIES	45
CABINETS DESIGNED TO SET FLUSH WITH THE CEILING HAVE A VISIBLE GAP, SPACE, OR SEPARATION	45
CABINETS ARE NOT SET *FLUSH* WITH ONE ANOTHER	45
CABINETS ARE WARPED	45
CABINET DRAWER GUIDE HAS BROKEN	46
CABINET DRAWER IS BINDING DURING OPENING	46
CABINET DOOR SWING OPEN AND / OR WILL NOT STAY CLOSED	46
DOORS OR DRAWERS HAVE CRACKS IN THE PANELS	47
PLASTIC LAMINATE SURFACES ARE PEELING AWAY	47

CABINETS DO NOT SIT LEVEL	47
CABINET DOORS DO NOT ALIGN WHEN CLOSED	48
CABINET FINISH (PAINT OR STAIN) IS IRREGULAR, MISMATCHED, OR BLOTCHY	48
GAPS APPEAR BETWEEN SECTIONS WHERE CABINETS ARE JOINED	48
STAIN GRADE CABINETS SHOW A "DARK" BAND AROUND DOOR AND DRAWER OPENINGS	48
MIRRORS	49
SCRATCHES ON GLASS SURFACE	49
MIRROR BACKING IS DETERIORATING	49
MIRROR WARDROBE DOORS DO NOT HAVE SAFETY BACKING (WALK-IN CLOSETS)	50
SHOWER AND TUB ENCLOSURES	50
GLASS/PLASTIC IS SCRATCHED	50
SHOWER OR TUB ENCLOSURES LEAK	50
FIBERGLASS OR ACRYLIC TUB BOTTOM OR SHOWER STALL ENCLOSURE FLEXES WHEN OCCUPIED	51
SHOWER/TUB ENCLOSURES ARE NOT TEMPERED GLASS	51
TOP RAIL OF SHOWER/TUB ENCLOSURE IS NOT SCREWED TO THE FRAME	51
GROUT IS CRACKED BETWEEN THE TUB/SHOWER AND FIRST ROW OF TILE	52
WATER RESISTANT BACKING IMPROPERLY INSTALLED AT TUB OR SHOWER SURROUNDINGS	52
ELECTRICAL	52
LIGHTS FLICKER WHEN APPLIANCES ARE TURNED ON	52
BREAKERS TRIP OR FUSES BLOW FREQUENCY	53
GROUND FAULT INTERRUPTER TRIPS FREQUENTLY	53
ALUMINUM WIRE, NOT COPPER WIRE, WAS INSTALLED	53
LIGHT FIXTURES TARNISH	54
LIGHT SWITCHES AND OUTLET PLATES PROTRUDE TOO FAR FROM WALL	54
LIGHT SWITCHES STICK OR MUST BE JIGGLED TO TURN THE LIGHT ON	54
WALL OUTLET IN BEDROOM DOES NOT WORK	55
BATHROOM FANS / LAUNDRY FANS ARE NOISY	55
PLUMBING	55
WATER OR GAS PIPING LEAKS	55

WATER PIPES FREEZE	56
WATER TASTES FUNNY, SMELLS, OR IS DISCOLORED	56
TOLIET BACKS UP, DRAINS BACK UP	57
INADEQUATE WATER PRESSURE	57
SEWER GAS SMELL COMING FROM DRAIN	58
COPPER WATER PIPES OR BLACK GAS PIPES ARE WET ON THE OUTSIDE	58
FAUCETS DRIP	58
SINK/TUB IS CHIPPED	59
SHOWER HEAD PIPE/TUB SPOUT IS LOOSE	59
FIBERGLASS TUB/SHOWER FLEXES WHEN OCCUPIED	59
WATER DRAINS FROM SINK/TUB WHEN STOPPED IS ENGAGED	59
BRASS BATHROOM FAUCETS AND DRAINS TARNISH	60
TOLIET RUNS CONTINUOUSLY	60
TOLIET LEAKS AT FLOOR	61
LACK OF HOT WATER	61
WATER HEATER IS NOT EARTHQUAKE SECURED, AS REQUIRED	62
ELECTRIC WATER HEATER CIRCUIT BREAKER TRIPS CONTINUOUSLY	62

MATERIAL CHARACTERISTICS AND MAINTENANCE GUIDELINES

APPLIANCES	63
MATERIAL CHARACTERISTICS	63
MAINTENANCE GUIDELINES	65
CABINETS	65
MATERIAL CHARACTERISTICS	65
MAINTENANCE GUIDELINES	66
COUNTERTOPS—CERAMIC TILE	67
MATERIAL CHARACTERISTICS	67
MAINTENANCE GUIDELINES	69
COUTERTOPS—CULTURED MARBLE	70
MATERIAL CHARACTERISTICS	70
MAINTENANCE GUIDELINES	70
COUNTERTOPS—MANUFACTURED SOLID SURFACE	71
MATERIAL CHARACTERISTICS	71
MATERIAL GUIDELINES	71
COUNTERTOPS—MARBLE AND STONE	71
MATERIAL CHARACTERISTICS	71
MAINTENANCE GUIDELINES	74

ELECTRICAL	76
MATERIAL CHARACTERISTICS	76
MAINTENANCE GUIDELINES	77
FLOORING-GENERAL	78
MATERIAL CHARACTERISTICS	78
MATERIAL GUIDELINES	79
FLOORING-CARPET	79
MATERIAL CHARACTERISTICS	79
MAINTENANCE GUIDELINES	80
FLOORING-CERAMIC TILE	82
MATERIAL CHARACTERISTICS	82
MAINTENANCE GUIDELINES	83
FLOORING-MARBLE AND STONE	84
MATERIAL CHARACTERISTICS	84
MAINTENANCE GUIDELINES	86
FLOORING-VINYL	88
MATERIAL CHARACTERISTICS	88
MAINTENANCE GUIDELINES	88
FLOORING – WOOD	90
MATERIAL CHARACTERISTICS	90
MAINTENANCE GUIDELINES	91
FOOD DISPOSAL	92
MATERIAL CHARACTERISTICS	92
MAINTENANCE GUIDELINES	92
OPERATING GUIDELINES	93
PAINTED SURFACES – INTERIOR	94
MATERIAL CHARACTERISTICS	94
MAINTENANCE GUIDELINES	95
PLUMBING - FAUCETS	96
MATERIAL CHARACTERISTICS	96
MAINTENANCE GUIDELINES	97
PLUMBING-PORCELAIN FIXTURES	97
MATERIAL CHARACTERISTICS	97
MAINTENANCE GUIDELINES	98
PLUMBING – TUB & SHOWER	98
MATERIAL CHARACTERISTICS	98
MAINTENANCE GUIDELINES	99
SHOWER ENCLOSURE	100
MATERIAL CHARACTERISTICS	100
MAINTENANCE GUIDELINES	101

SHOWER WALLS – CERAMIC TILE	101
MATERIAL CHARACTERISTICS	101
MAINTENANCE GUIDELINES	102
SMOKE DETECTORS	102
MATERIAL CHARACTERISTICS	102
MAINTENANCE GUIDELINES	104

HOMEOWNER MAINTENANCE TIPS

Drains	107
Drywall	107
Electrical	107
Fencing	108
Garage Doors	109
BIBLIOGRAPHY AND REFERENCES	113

QUALITY INSPECTION CHECKLIST

CABINETS

Pre-Work Inspection: (to be completed prior to beginning work)
Date Completed _____

___ Color selection sheet(s) has been received by Contractor.

___ Cabinet areas are field-measured (after drywall has been installed).

___ Windows are intact with none broken.

___ Tubs are covered and undamaged.

___ Temporary stairs (if required), temporary handrails, and safety bracing are installed.

___ House is broom-swept, clean, and free of debris

Final Inspection: (to be completed before Trade Contractor leaves jobsite)   Date Completed _____

___ Windows are intact with none broken.

___ Temporary handrails, safety bracing, etc., are intact.

___ Cabinets are installed per plan (correct number, size, etc.).

___ Cabinets are level and plumb.

___ Cabinets are secured correctly and tightly to wall.

___ Color of cabinets and countertops is correct.

___ Colored caulk is used if colored cabinets and countertops.

___ Cabinet doors and drawer fronts are level and square.

___ Cabinet faces and corners are level and plumb.

___ All doors and drawers open and close correctly.

___ Correct hardware is installed—square, plumb, and correctly.

___ Screws attaching hardware have not splintered wood.

___ Kick plates are installed with no gaps or holes.

___ HVAC vent is cut correctly (if required). Shoe molding will fit below vent.

___ Cabinets are undamaged.

___ Cabinets are intact with no unfilled holes.

___ Shelves are level and undamaged.

___ The number of shelves is correct.

___   For adjustable shelves, all holders fit, none are missing, and are level.

___   For all rollout shelves, operation is smooth and shelves track tight and secure.

___   Lazy susan(s) are installed plumb, work correctly, and are secured tightly.

___ Cabinets are clean inside and out.

___ Countertops are protected with cardboard that is taped securely.

___ House is clean, broom-swept, and debris removed.

QUALITY INSPECTION CHECKLIST

COUNTER TOPS

Pre-Work Inspection: (to be completed prior to beginning work)
Date Completed _____

___ Color, and material selection sheet has been given to Contractor.

___ Cabinet areas have been field-measured.

___ Windows are intact with none broken.

___ Tubs are covered and undamaged.

___ Temporary stairs, if required, temporary handrails, and safety bracing are installed.

___ House is broom-swept, clean, and free of debris.

Final Inspection: (to be completed before Trade Contractor leaves jobsite)   Date Completed _____

___ Windows are intact with none broken.

___ Temporary handrails, safety bracing, etc., are intact.

___ Counter tops are installed per plan (correct number, size, material, color, etc.).

___ Tops are level and plumb.

___ Tops are secured correctly and tightly to wall.

___ Color(s) of counter tops are correct.

___ Counter tops are undamaged.

___ Counter tops are protected with cardboard and taped securely.

___ House is clean, broom-swept, and debris has been removed.

QUALITY INSPECTION CHECKLIST

ELECTRIC (FINAL)

Pre-Work Inspection: (to be completed prior to beginning work)
Date Completed _____

___ House is clean and free of debris.

___ Drywall is complete with no damage.

___ Painting is complete with no damage.

___ All receptacle boxes are clean and free of drywall mud and other debris.

___ House is at stage for final electrical to be completed.

___ House is broom-swept, clean, and free of debris.

Final Inspection: (to be completed before Trade Contractor leaves jobsite)   Date Completed _____

___ All faceplates are installed square, plumb, and snug against walls.

___ All receptacles are tested and all work as required.

___ All appliances are hooked up and tested.

___ Garbage disposal is tested.

___ All light fixtures are installed and tested.

___ Smoke detectors are hooked up and tested.

___ Bath fans and ceiling fans are hooked up and tested.

___ Outdoor boxes must be weatherproofed.

___ House and Site are clean and free of debris.

QUALITY INSPECTION CHECKLIST

FLOOR COVERINGS

Initial Inspection (prior to installing parquet, hardwood, or vinyl flooring): (to be completed prior to beginning work)
Date Completed _____

___ Color selection has been verified.

___ Jobsite is clean and free of debris.

___ House is clean and broom-swept.

___ Driveway is clean and barricaded.

___ Temporary handrails, bracing, etc., are in place.

___ Floor is level with no more than 1/4 inch in 32-inches deviation.

___ Floor is clean.

___ Subflooring cracks are filled and sanded level.

___ No bumps, overlaps, etc., are in subfloor or slab.

___ Subflooring or slab is dry.

Final Inspection (after installing parquet, hardwood, or vinyl flooring): (to be completed before Trade Contractor leaves jobsite)
Date Completed _____

___ Floors are level after installation of floor covering with no deviation more than 1/4 inch in 32 inches.

___ Floor coverings are cut within 1/8 inch of wall.

___ Floor coverings are firmly attached with no bubbles, nail pops, lumps, bumps, etc.

___ Pattern of vinyl is laid square, and correct, and in a manner that helps diminish any wall deflections.

___ Floor coverings are correct at door casings. Subflooring or slab is not visible.

___ Floor coverings are correct at toilets.

___ Vinyl is flush with cabinets and tubs.

___ Floor coverings are correct at all ducts.

___ Hardwood flooring does not have gaps, splinters, or loose areas.

___ Tile, hardwood, and vinyl flooring has been inspected under normal interior lighting and also in sunlight from windows. No defects were found.

___ Floor coverings are protected from damage.

___ House is clean with all working areas broom-swept.

___ Debris and trash have been removed to designated trash site.

___ Left-over vinyl, tile, tile grout, and hardwood flooring has been stacked in the garage, store room, or laundry area.

QUALITY INSPECTION CHECKLIST

MIRRORS

Pre-Work Inspection: (to be completed prior to beginning work)
Date Completed _____

___ Contractor has specifications for mirrors, has ordered mirrors, and has an expected delivery date.

___ Drywall and painting are complete, and have had sufficient time to dry. Never install mirrors on unsealed/unpainted wall.

___ Cabinets are installed.

___ Drywall and paint are undamaged.

___ Counter tops are installed, undamaged, and protected.

___ Windows are installed and undamaged.

___ House is clean, broom-swept, and free of debris.

Final Inspection: (to be completed before Trade Contractor leaves jobsite)   Date Completed _____

___ All windows are intact and unbroken.

___ Drywall and paint are undamaged.

___ Countertops are undamaged and remain protected.

___ Mirror installers wear gloves to prevent damage from skin-borne salts or chemicals from coming into contact with mirror backing.

___ Mirror is installed at least 3/8" above closest surface to bottom of mirror. Never install mirror in contact with counter top/back splash.

___ Mirrors are installed level, plumb, and square by 1/8" per 6 feet.

___ Mirrors are installed into solid backing, per plan and per specification.

___ J-Channel has weep holes (if used).

___ Mirror has 3mm neoprene setting pads between the mirror and clip/channel.

___ Mirrors are undamaged with no visible imperfections, peeling, flaking, chips, cracks, scratches, discoloration, or damage to backing under normal lighting conditions from a 3 foot distance.

___ Adhesives (if used) should be a "neutral-cure" product. Avoid adhesives with solvents like acetone, toluene, methylene chloride, acetic acid, etc.

___ Mirrors are installed per manufacturer's recommendations.

___ House is clean and broom-swept, and debris has been removed.

QUALITY INSPECTION CHECKLIST

PAINTING (FINAL)

Pre-Work Inspection: (to be completed prior to beginning work)
Date Completed _____

___ There is no damage to tubs, showers, countertops, stairs, cabinets, windows, flooring, etc.

___ All protective coverings are in place (tubs, countertops, flooring, etc.).

___ All drywall repairs have been completed, surface is smooth and sanded with no raised facepaper from over-sanding.

___ Wall texture is consistent throughout.

___ All damaged trim has been repaired or replaced.

___ There is no carpet on the floor.

___ House is ready to be painted.

___ House is clean, broom-swept, and free of debris.

Final Inspection: (to be completed before Trade Contractor leaves jobsite)   Date Completed _____

___ Second coat of paint applied to walls is smooth, with no runs, drips, lumps, color variations, streaking, or light spots.

___ Second coat of trim paint applied to trim and doors is smooth, with no runs, drips, lumps, color variations, streaking, or light spots.

___ All stairs and handrails are stained or painted per plan.

___ All stained areas have a uniform appearance and complete coverage.

___ Varnish is applied smoothly and uniformly to all stained areas.

___ There is no damage to drywall, stairs, handrails, trim, etc.

___ Paint spills have been **removed without damage** to vinyl, wood floors, tubs, showers, countertops, etc.

___ Paint has been removed from window glass and frames.

___ Paint has been removed from door hinges and all hardware.

___ Doors have been rehung, and are square, level, plumb, and back where they belong.

___ Thresholds are painted/stained at all exterior doors.

___ No defects are visible under sunlight and normal house lighting from a distance of 6 feet for the entire interior paint job.

___ There is no paint residue in sinks.

___ Interior walls are smooth with no drips, runs, lumps, bumps, color variations, or streaking.

___ Interior walls have uniform coverage after first coat is sprayed.

___ All rough spots have been repaired in interior trim. Nail holes are filled and sanded smooth.

___ First coat trim paint applied.

___ Inside of HVAC cans/boots are painted black.

___ Six sides of each door has been painted (including top and bottom).

___ Excess trim paint on walls has been cleaned off.

___ Over-spray has been cleaned from windows (glass and frames).

___ Paint buckets, sprayers, etc. are not set on top of finished surfaces, ie. Countertops, flooring, tubs, garage floors, drive, patio, deck, etc.

___ There is no damage to finished surfaces from spills, drips, etc.

___ There is no damage to cabinets or countertops.

___ All interior wood is caulked.

___ Tubs, sinks, showers, flooring, etc., have no damage.

___ Empty paint buckets are removed from site.

___ Paint brushes, sprayers, buckets, etc. do not get washed out in sinks, gutters, landscape, etc.

___ No debris in garages.

___ Debris has been removed to the dumpster.

___ House is clean and broom-swept.

QUALITY INSPECTION CHECKLIST

PAINTING (ROUGH)

Pre-Work Inspection: (to be completed prior to beginning work)
Date Completed _____

___ Plans, specifications, and colors have been reviewed with Contractor.
___ Windows are intact with none broken.
___ Flooring is protected.
___ Tubs, showers, countertops, etc., are protected.
___ All drywall is installed, taped, mudded, and sanded.
___ Texture is complete and consistent throughout.
___ Drywall is straight with no bows or depressions.
___ Joints in drywall are smooth and clean.
___ Drywall has no excessive nicks, gouges, scrapes, etc.
___ Drywall has no raised face-paper from over-sanding.
___ Corners have no hairline cracks.
___ Drywall has no nail pops or loose nails.
___ Trim fits properly around all windows and doors
___ Paint grade window and door casing, crown molding, chair rail, have been caulked and nail holes are filled and sanded.
___ Baseboard has no nicks, gouges, scratches, damage, etc.
___ Nails are set properly in baseboard at correct depth with no protruding nails.
___ Baseboard is secured tightly, corners are correct and tight.
___ Baseboard around cabinets is tacked in place.
___ All doors are installed according to plan, and are plumb, square, the proper distance for carpet or vinyl, and swing correctly.
___ All bifold doors are square, plumb, and tracks are installed tightly.
___ Attic accesses are installed correctly and all trim is in place.
___ There is no missing trim in any room.
___ Chair rail or crown is installed, if required by plan or options.

___ House is broom-swept, clean, and free of debris.

Final Inspection: (to be completed before Trade Contractor leaves jobsite)   Date Completed _____

___ Exterior wall paint has uniform coverage, and no light spots.

___ Exterior trim paint has uniform coverage, uniform color, and no paint of walls.

___ Exterior metal painted uniform color and no paint on walls/roof tile

___ Exterior paint job inspected from 6-foot distance (entire job) with no visible defects.

___ No paint is on windows, brick, stucco, doors, concrete flatwork, or other areas.

___ Metal lintels are clean (no rust) and painted black with rust-proof paint.

___ All exterior wood is caulked.

___ All gaps between the brickmold and brick are caulked.

___ All thresholds are caulked.

___ Windows are intact with none broken.

___ Paint is stored properly.

___ MSDS sheets displayed.

___ No debris in garages.

___ Empty paint buckets are picked up and removed from jobsite.

QUALITY INSPECTION CHECKLIST

PAINTING (TOUCH-UP)

Pre-Work Inspection: (to be completed prior to beginning work)
Date Completed _____

___ All work by other trade contractors is complete, except the cleaning crew.

Final Inspection: (to be completed before Trade Contractor leaves jobsite)   Date Completed _____

___ All areas of paint have been inspected and no missed repairs were found.

___ Touch-up paint areas blend with surrounding areas (no difference visible from 6 feet in sunlight from windows and under normal house lighting).

___ No excess paint is on any area (windows, trim, doors, floors, etc.).

___ Correct colors & sheens were used. i.e. Flat pain is not used to touch up in areas painted with semi-gloss paint, etc.

___ House is clean and free of debris, and ready for the cleaning crew.

QUALITY INSPECTION CHECKLIST

PLUMBING (FINAL)

Pre-Work Inspection: (to be completed prior to beginning work)
Date Completed _____

___ House is clean and free of debris from prior trade contractors.
___ Windows are intact and unbroken.
___ Flooring in water closets are installed and undamaged.
___ Tub(s) is undamaged.
___ Cabinets are installed.
___ Gas test has been completed (after cabinets have been installed).
___ Correct dimensions for water closets (walls, cabinets, etc.) are verified.
___ All safety bracing, temporary handrails, etc., are in place, if required.

Final Inspection: (to be completed before Trade Contractor leaves jobsite)   Date Completed _____

___ All fixtures are set, and are not tarnished, chipped, or otherwise defective.
___ All fixtures and faucets (brand and type) correspond to plans and specifications.
___ All fixtures have been tested for operation.
___ Garbage disposal operates smoothly.
___ Dishwasher operates evenly, with no leaks. Run through entire cycle.
___ There are no scratches, dents, or chipped surfaces on appliances.
___ No leaks have been found.
___ Toilets are placed, level, and caulked after finished floor is installed.
___ Toilets are operational, adjusted correctly and do not continuously run, or seep.

___ Test all fixtures for filling and draining. Drains shall flow freely.
___ Turn on all sink faucets and flush all toilets at the same time to see if they'll all work without a major reduction in water flow.
___ Turn on faucets, tubs, and drains on upper floors. See if any stains from on downstairs ceiling beneath those fixtures.
___ No excessive noise is heard from water pipes.
___ No water hammering when shutting off water.
___ No surface defects in faucets, tubs or showers have been found.
___ Tub(s) and shower(s) are fully secured to wall.
___ Showerhead pipes, tub spouts, etc. should be secured and should not move in or out.
___ If pedestal sink, water shutoff valves are accessible and usable.
___ All faucets and showerheads are in alignment (level and straight).
___ Regular water shutoffs are all accessible and in working order.
___ Correct number of water shutoffs have been verified.
___ Turn on all outdoor spigots. Make sure they close easily and completely.
___ Water shutoff at street works correctly.
___ Water meter box is installed level, and is not located in drainage swale.
___ Hot and cold water are identified at each shutoff valve (including clothes washer shutoff).
___ Hot water is on the left, cold on the right.
___ Correct number of outside faucets have been verified and all are working.
___ Strainer and stopper are in good condition and placed in drawer in kitchen.

___ Emergency key for garbage disposal is in drawer in kitchen with strainer and stopper.

___ Warranty and instruction manuals for hot water heater and garbage disposal are in kitchen drawer to left of range.

___ Hot water heater works (checked at each faucet) and is installed per manufacturer's instructions.

___ Water heater tank has a TPRV (Temperature Pressure Relief Valve) discharge pipe installed.

___ Test the TPRV to see if it opens easily and seals shut when closed.

___ Water heater drain pan and discharge pipe installed, if required.

___ Water heater's manufacturers identification label in on water heater. Should identify manufacturer, model number, serial number, date manufactured, etc.

___ Anti-siphon valves, vacuum relief valves/vacuum breakers, backflow preventers, etc. are installed as required.

___ All inspections have been passed.

___ House and site are clean, broom-swept, and free of debris.

QUALITY INSPECTION CHECKLIST

SHOWER DOORS

Pre-Work Inspection: (to be completed prior to beginning work)
Date Completed _____

___ Plans, specifications, and colors have been verified.

___ Shower is installed and ready for shower doors.

___ Windows are installed and undamaged.

___ House is clean, broom-swept, and free of debris.

Final Inspection: (to be completed before Trade Contractor leaves jobsite)   Date Completed _____

___ All windows are intact and unbroken.

___ Shower stall is undamaged.

___ Shower doors are installed level, plumb, square, and operate smoothly.

___ Shower doors are installed per plan.

___ House is clean and broom-swept.

___ Debris has been removed to correct area.

QUALITY INSPECTION CHECKLIST

TRIM LABOR

Pre-Work Inspection: (to be completed prior to beginning work) Date Completed _____

___ Material is on site and ready to be used.

___ House is clean, broom-swept, and free of debris.

___ Garage is clean.

___ Windows are intact and unbroken.

___ Stairs are installed.

___ Drywall is undamaged.

___ Vinyl is undamaged.

___ Ducts are covered.

___ Tubs are covered and undamaged.

___ Sinks, cabinets, and countertops are covered and undamaged.

___ Cabinets are set.

___ Doors are framed plumb and of correct size. Plan used to check carpet and vinyl areas.

___ Swing of doors is clearly marked on inside of each doorjamb.

___ Disappearing stairs are installed, if required.

___ Attic access is framed.

Final Inspection: (to be completed before Trade Contractor leaves job site)   Date Completed _____

___ Windows are intact and unbroken.

___ Drywall is undamaged.

___ Vinyl is undamaged.

___ Ducts are covered.

___ Tubs are covered and undamaged.

___ Sinks, cabinets, and countertops are covered and undamaged.

___ Base molding is installed securely to walls.

___ Base molding is undamaged and all nicks, gouges, etc., are repaired and sanded.

___ Base molding is level and straight, especially in tight and/or short runs.

___ Crown if required, is secure, level, and straight.

___ Chair rails, if required, are secure, level, and straight.

___ Nail holes are correct depth with no splintering or cracking.

___ Corners are cut correctly and fit snugly.

___ Doors are hung level, plumb, and shimmed.

___ Door/Window casing is secure, level, and straight.

___ Handrails are installed to the correct length, and are straight and secure.

___ Pickets and newels are installed correctly and securely with no movement.

___ Shoe molding is installed over all vinyl, securely and tightly to the base.

___ Shoe molding cuts at doors are cut 1/4 inch or less.

___ Corners of shoe molding fit snugly and are cut correctly.

___ Stair treads are undamaged.

___ Attic access areas are trimmed per plan.

___ Excess material has been removed to garage.

___ All debris has been removed to dumpster.

___ House is clean and broom-swept.

Common Remodeling Construction Defects

PAINT AND STAIN

STAINS FROM UNDERLYING SURFACES BLEED THROUGH

Colors, markings, wood sap, tannins, etc. which are on the surface of or are within the composition of underlying materials should not bleed through to the surface of the paint.

Resolution: Builder should ensure that surfaces to which paints and stains are applied are properly prepared and cleaned. If components of an underlying material have an inherent tendency to bleed through, The Builder should apply stain blocking coatings or primers before proceeding with painting or staining.

Recommendation: None.

PAINT BECOMES CHALKS OR FADES

Paint should not chalk or fade within the period of time that the manufacturer warrants its performance from such deterioration.

Resolution: Builder should select paints and stains that are suitable for the exposure and climate zone for the House.

Recommendation: It is important to observe the condition of painted surfaces on a periodic basis. An annual inspection is recommended. Paints first begin to show signs of wear in limited areas. Maintenance and touch up should be undertaken before paint degradation proceeds too far. This can significantly extend the life of the overall paint job.

PAINT FLAKING OR PEELING

Paint should not flake or peel during the manufacturer's warranted life of the product.

Resolution: Builder should ensure that appropriate paint selections are made, and that surfaces are properly prepared to receive paints. In the case of premature flaking or peeling, the Builder should take appropriate action to remediate the non-performing condition, up to and including stripping and repainting affected surfaces, as may be required to provide a durable finish.

Recommendation: Maintain paint surfaces in a clean and well-ventilated condition. Inspect painted surfaces periodically and touch up any initial onset of premature aging or deterioration that may be observed.

PAINTS APPLED TOO THIN, TOO TICK, OR IN A SPOTTY MANNER

All surfaces to receive pain should uniformly coated without any unpainted or too lightly painted spots called "holidays" in the painting trade. Paint coatings should be applied to at least the minimum thickness recommended by the manufacturer. Paint should not be applied too thick, which usually results in spots that are more reflective than surrounding surfaces called "shiners." Paint should be applied smoothly and evenly, without any runs or drips.

Resolution: The Builder should conform to the Performance Guideline. Any areas that are not painted in conformance to the Guideline should be repainted properly.

Recommendation: None.

PAINT OR STAIN OVERSPRAY ON ADJACENT SURFACES

Over spray of paints or stains on surfaces that are not intended to receive paint or stain coatings is not acceptable. Over spray must be clearly visible at a distance of five feet under normal natural lighting conditions to be non-performing.

Resolution: Builder should take measures to protect surfaces that are not to be painted and which may be subject to overspray damage. If overspray occurs despite protective measures, Builder should clean the affected areas in a manner that does not damage the affected surfaces.

Recommendation: None.

MILDEW OR FUNGI GROWTH / STAINS ON PAINTED SURFACES

Mildew and fungi that affect exterior surfaces may be difficult or impossible to avoid in some particularly moist and cool locations and therefore are not considered a condition of non-performance. Molds and mildews that appear on interior surfaces, and are the result of leaks, are considered unacceptable. Interior surfaces similarly affected by condensation may either be considered unacceptable or a Homeowner maintenance item, depending upon circumstances.

Resolution: Builder is responsible for selection of paints that are reasonably resistant to the establishment and spread of mildews and fungi on exterior walls. Paints are now formulated with mildewcide and fungicide additives that inhibit the growth of mildew and fungi. The Builder should use these types of products on exterior walls when the orientation and climate at the home site indicates their use is necessary. At interior walls, if mildews and molds become established as a consequence of leaks in the exterior walls, roof above, or any other building component, it should be the Builder's responsibility to correct the leaks, and to clean up and restore any affected areas (if leaks are a result of improper construction).

Recommendation: Homeowner should periodically inspect exterior surfaces to determine if mildew or fungus growth is occurring. Any growth of these organisms should be addressed by the proper cleaning and application of products that will kill the organisms and retard their return. This should be done promptly upon observation of mildews or fungi, because once established, these organisms are progressively more difficult to control and eradicate. At interior locations, the Homeowner should always use the mechanical ventilation in bathrooms, laundry rooms, and kitchens while these rooms are in use, and regularly air out rooms that have windows. If the Homeowner observes significant condensation on exterior surfaces (usually at windows and cool exterior walls), an effort should be made to find the right balance of natural and mechanical ventilation to minimize the problem.

LACQUERS AND VARNISHES PEEL AND FLAKE RAPIDLY

Clear exterior lacquer and varnish coatings are not recommended for use on exterior surfaces. They usually deteriorate rapidly and require substantial maintenance. Deteriorated exterior varnishes and lacquers are not considered acceptable. Interior varnished and lacquered surfaces may be appropriate, provided that they are not applied in locations subject to extensive direct sunlight or excessive moisture.

Resolution: Interior lacquers and varnishes that peel or flake off, and are not subject to Homeowner abuse or excessive moisture, should be corrected by the Builder.

Recommendation: Homeowner should keep all varnished and lacquered surfaces reasonably free of excessive moisture, heat, dust, and from other damaging conditions. Relatively frequent maintenance and recoating with a high quality marine spray varnish should be anticipated and performed by the Homeowner.

STAINED EXTERIOR SURFACES ARE BLOTCHY OR HAVE UNEVEN COLOR

Stains are absorbed by wood to different degrees, depending on the prevalence of sapwood, knots, and the character of the tree from which the wood product was made, Stains on synthetic surfaces may be more regular, but some variation is still inevitable. Stained surfaces, however, should not be excessively blotchy, or vary markedly in color.

Resolution: Builder should prepare surfaces and apply stains in strict accordance with the manufacturer's directions and recommendations, and in a manner that minimizes extreme variations in color or blotchiness. Surfaces that are not in conformance should be cleaned and re-coated in a manner that achieves a reasonable degree of regularity.

Recommendation: Homeowner is responsible for maintaining the stained surfaces clean and free of debris. Adequate ventilation of exposed surfaces should be provided. Homeowner should recoat stained surfaces at an interval no longer than what is recommended by the manufacturer.

PAINTED STUCCO SURFACES DO NOT PERMIT MOISTURE TO ESCAPE

Stucco surfaces that are designed to receive paint should be painted with materials that allow water vapor to pass from the inner surface to the outer surface. The use of impermeable membrane paints in considered unacceptable for this application.

Resolution: Apply only breathable surface coatings to stucco exteriors. Apply according to the methods and thickness recommended by the manufacturer.

Recommendation: None.

BRUSH MARKS OR LAP MARKS SHOW

When viewed in normal daylight at a distance of 6 feet, brush marks or lap marks should not be visible. Artificial light is not acceptable as a light source when measuring this Guideline.

Resolution: Builder should make corrections to non-conforming items.

Recommendation: None.

FINISH FLOORING

FLOOR NOT LEVEL, FLOOR SQUEAKS, EXCESSIVE DEFLECTION (SAGGING), EXCESSIVE FELEXIBILITY (BOUNCE)

Finish floors should not deviate more than 1/4-inch from true level in a horizontal distance of 8 feet. No point in the surface of a floor should be more than 1/8-inch above or below the plane of the floor. Squeaks are usually the result of separate parts of the floor moving relative to each other and rubbing against nails. Floors should be designed to accommodate Building Code required live loads.

Resolution: Builder should repair or replace finish flooring that deviates from the above guideline, if condition is a result of improper or inadequate installation and not a result of Homeowner misuse.

Recommendation: Maintain flooring using products and methods approved by the manufacturer and/ or trade association whose products have been installed. Avoid overloading floors. Consult with the Builder or a qualified engineer prior to placing exceptionally heavy objects on a floor to ensure the floor load capacity will not be exceeded. If the Homeowner installs a finish floor, the Homeowner assumes complete responsibility for the conation of the subfloor or slab at the time of installation and thereafter.

HARDWOOD FLOORING

CUPPING OR CROWNING OF INDIVIDUAL FLOOR BOARDS

Hardwood flooring should be installed in a manner that will prevent cupping and crowning. This includes, among other measures, proper acclimatization of floor material prior to installation and the use of suitable moisture barriers under the flooring. Cupping or crowning should not exceed 1/16-inch in a 3-inch span as measured across the individual board.

Resolution: If cupping or crowning exceeds the Guideline, the Builder should replace or repair the floor as necessary to meet the Guideline.

Recommendation: Always maintain hardwood floor in accordance with the manufacturer's recommendations, do not allow any spills or liquids to remain on floors, and do not clean floors with detergents. Use only those cleaning products recommended by the manufacturer. Some minor random cupping or crowning can be expected over the years due to changes in humidity, and this condition is acceptable.

SCALLEOPED AND ABRADED SURFACE

Wood floors should be finished without gouges, abrasions or scalloping. Some unevenness can be expected because portions of the grain of wood are softer than others.

Resolution: Builder should repair or replace any non-performing boards noticed at the Walkthrough.

Recommendation: Any surface gouges and abrasions should be brought to the attention of the Builder at the Walkthrough and prior to the move-in. The Builder is not responsible for gouges and abrasions noticed after the Walkthrough. Always maintain hardwood floor in accordance with the manufacturer's recommendations, do not allow any spills or liquids to remain on floors, and do not clean floors with detergents. Use only those cleaning products recommended by the manufacturer.

GAPS BETWEEN ADJACENT FLOOR BOARDS

Manufactured (pre-finished) floors should be installed strictly in accordance with the manufacturer's instructions and should perform in accordance with the manufacturer's warranty. Floors finished in the field: floor joints should be tight and without gaps. Gaps between boards are the result of shrinkage. Although wood flooring materials are dried by the manufacturer, they still contain moisture. New wood floors should not be subjected to extreme variations in temperature or humidity. Gaps should not occur in more than 5% of the total length of joints in a floor, and no gap should exceed 1/32-inch in width for boards in excess of 2-1/4-inches in width.

Resolution: If gaps between boards exceed the Guideline, the Builder should replace or repair the floor as necessary to meet the Guideline.

Recommendation: Always maintain hardwood floor in accordance with the manufacturer's recommendations, do not allow any spills or liquids to remain on floors, and do not clean floors with detergents. Use only those cleaning products recommended by the manufacturer.

DIFFERENCES IN COLOR BETWEEN INDIVIDUAL FLOOR BOARDS

Wood floors naturally have color variation. The same species of wood may come in many different colors, floor boards may vary accordingly.

Resolution: None.

Recommendation: If uniformity of color is important, Homeowner should make advance arrangement with the Builder at the time the flooring section is completed, so that the Homeowner is present when the floor is being installed. Homeowner should be aware that direct sunlight can cause wood floors to become lighter; the Builder is not responsible for this condition. The floor areas under area rugs and large pieces of furniture will remain as the original wood or stain color (usually darker). Removal of the rug or relocation of the furniture will allow the floor to reach a uniform color.

FLOOR BOARDS ON PRE-FINISHED FLOORS ARE NOT LEVEL WITH ONE ANOTHER AT SIDES OR ENDS

Finish floorboards should not be higher or lower than the immediately adjoining board by more than .012-inch measured with a feeler gauge.

Resolution: Builder should make necessary repairs to meet the above guideline, unless condition is a result of a Homeowner misuse or improper maintenance.

Recommendation: Floor care is important. If water based liquid is spilled on the floor, or if areas of high humidity exist in poorly vented rooms, the floorboards may swell and become uneven. Builder is not responsible for this condition.

SPLINTERS OR CHIPS ARE PRESENT AT THE EDGES OF FLOOR BOARDS AFTER INSTALLATION

Whether the floor is pre-finished or sanded and finished in place, there should be no splinters or chips that could be caught in flesh or clothing after installation is complete.

Resolution: Repair or replace boards that do not meet the above guideline.

Recommendation: Floor care is important. Always maintain hardwood floor in accordance with the manufacturer's recommendations, do not allow any spills or liquids to remain on floors, and do not clean floors with detergents. Use only those cleaning products recommended by the manufacturer.

DARK LINES APPEAR PERPENDICULAR TO THE FLOOR BOARD

Sticker lines across floorboards that cannot be removed during the sanding process are considered unacceptable. To be considered unacceptable, the dark line should be clearly visible to the untrained eye at a distance of 6 feet under normal daylight conditions

Resolution: Replace or replace floorboards that do not meet the above Performance Guideline.

Recommendation: Always maintain hardwood floor in accordance with the manufacturer's recommendations, do not allow any spills or liquids to remain on floors, and do not clean floors with detergents. Use only those cleaning products recommended by the manufacturer.

FLOOR BOARDS DISCOLOR AND ROT, PARTICULARLY UNDER AREA RUGS

Floorboards should not discolor (turn very dark) and rot, or become brittle and crumble.

Resolution: Builder should make repairs unless the damage is caused by Homeowner misuse or negligence.

Recommendation: If the Homeowner covers a pre-finished hardwood floor with an area rug, he or she takes on the responsibility to monitor the condition of the wood on a quarterly basis (every three months). To avoid this, the area rug can be installed on the concrete slab with the wood floor around it. Homeowner should also be aware that direct sunlight will cause wood floors to become darker; the Builder is not responsible for this condition.

CERAMIC AND CLAY TILE FLOORING

CRACKS AND / OR LOOSE TILES

Tiles having cracks that are visible at a distance of 4 feet, and any loose tiles that can be moved by hand, are not acceptable.

Resolution: Builder should replace cracked tiles and reset loose tiles that do not meet the above guideline.

Recommendation: Homeowner should be aware that ceramic and clay tiles are brittle and they can be cracked, chipped or broken by placing or dropping heavy objects on them; the Builder is not responsible for the resulting conditions.

GROUT IS CRACKED

Hairline cracks can occur in grout and are considered acceptable. Cracks larger than 1/32 inch should be re-grouted as part of the Builder's Responsibility. If continual cracking occurs, the underlying floor may be deflecting. If this condition exists, it should be repaired.

Resolution: Builder should meet the Performance guideline by repairing or replacing any non-performing condition.

Recommendation: Homeowners should familiarize themselves with proper procedures for cleaning and caring for their tile floors. Grout is very porous and should be sealed by the Homeowner within 30 days of occupancy.

INDIVIDUAL TILES ARE OUT OF PLANE

This Guideline will vary depending upon the type of tile that is installed. Tiles can vary from flat ceramic, to rose, to uneven terra cotta. For tile that is flat, adjoining tiles should be no more than 1/16-inch higher or lower than the surrounding tiles. For tile that is handmade with uneven surfaces, the butts at the grout joints should not exceed 1/4-inch in elevation from surrounding tiles.

Resolution: Builder should repair or replace any non-performing tiles.

Recommendation: Homeowners should familiarize themselves with proper procedures for cleaning and caring for their tile floors.

GRANITE, MARBLE, AND OTHER STONE FLOORING

CRACKS

Granite, marble, and other stone are susceptible to hairline cracking. This is normal condition. Cracks in excess of 3/64-inch are unacceptable.

Resolution: Builder should repair or replace any non-conforming condition that is a result of initial construction, and is not a product of Homeowner misuse.

Recommendation: Examine floors carefully at time of the Walkthrough. Homeowner should not place unusually heavy items onto stone flooring, unless Builder was notified and has provided appropriate support.

STAINS

Builder should deliver a marble, granite, or other stone floor free of stains, with a consistent surface sheen or texture. The Homeowner should carefully examine the surface of the marble, granite, or other stone floor prior to taking possession of the House. The Builder will not accept responsibility for stained conditions if they are not noted at the time of the Walkthrough. Many times what may appear to be discolorations are actually natural variations in the stone.

Resolution: Builder should repair or replace the non-conforming condition if noted at the time of the Walkthrough.

Recommendation: None. Ensure that you careful examination of the floor during the Walkthrough.

SCRATCHES AND ABRASIONS

Homeowner should note any scratches and abrasions during the Walkthrough. The Builder should deliver a marble, granite, or other stone floor free of scratches and abrasions, with a consistent surface sheen or texture.

Resolution: Marble, granite, and tumbled stone will naturally have numerous pits and voids. Small pits are considered part of the "achieved look" of the surface and should not be deemed as non-preforming. The manufacturer or installer usually fills voids in excess of 3/8-inch in diameter.

Recommendation: None; careful examination of the floor during the Walkthrough.

VINYL FLOORING

WIDE SEAMS OR JOINTS

Sheet and tile resilient floors should be laid with tight joints. Any separation in excess of 1/32-inch is non-performing.

Resolution: Builder should make necessary repairs or replacements.

Recommendation: Homeowners should follow the flooring manufacturer's cleaning and care instructions for vinyl flooring.

DELAMINATION

Occasionally resilient floors will separate from the underlayment, particularly at edges. Such delamination is unacceptable and should be corrected by re-gluing.

Resolution: Builder should make necessary repairs or replacements.

Recommendation: Homeowners should follow the flooring manufacturer's cleaning and care instructions for vinyl flooring. To extend the life of vinyl flooring, use area rugs or mats at workstations and use dirt-trapping mats at exterior doors. Do not allow water or other liquids to remain on vinyl flooring for long periods of time. Spills or splashes should be promptly and properly removed. Vinyl flooring is water resistant and not totally waterproof.

DISCOLORATION

Floors should not become discolored as a result of moisture underneath the finish floor. If discoloration is a result of chemical and natural products with staining properties being allowed to remain on the surface of the resilient material without prompt cleaning, Builder is not responsible.

Resolution: Builder should make necessary repairs or replacements if condition is a result of moisture underneath the finish floor and not a result of Homeowner misuse or negligence.

Recommendation: Do not allow chemical or natural products with staining properties to remain on the finish floor. Homeowners should follow the flooring manufacturer's cleaning and care instructions for vinyl flooring. Do not allow water or other liquids to remain on vinyl flooring for long periods of time. Spills or splashes should be promptly and properly.

ADHESIVE APPEARS ON THE SURFACE THROUGH JOINTS

Adhesives should not appear through the surface around joints or seams.

Resolution: Builder should making necessary repairs or replacements. If after thorough cleaning with a manufacturer-approved cleaning agent the non-performing condition recurs, the floor should be removed along with the existing adhesive, and the floor re-laid by the Builder.

Recommendation: Homeowners should follow the flooring manufacturer's cleaning and care instructions for vinyl flooring.

"TELEGRAPHING" OR IRREGULAR SURFACE BEANEATH VINYL FLOORING

Various types of irregularities, such as cracks in concrete subfloors, or unevenness in subfloors, or trapped debris, may show through the resilient flooring observed at a distance of 6 ft. under normal lighting conditions, appearing as unsightly bumps and lines. These conditions are non-performing.

Resolution: Builder should making necessary repairs or replacements to non-performing conditions.

Recommendation: Homeowners should following the flooring manufacturer's cleaning and care instructions for vinyl flooring.

PATTERN DOES NOT MATCH OR ALIGN

Patterns should match or align within 1/8-inch in a six-foot length of flooring.

Resolution: Builder should make necessary repairs or replacements, assuming no damage or misuse by Homeowner.

Recommendation: Homeowners should follow the flooring manufacturer's cleaning and care instructions for vinyl flooring.

CARPET FLOORING

VISIBLE SEEMS

Visibility of carpet seams is acceptable unless the seam is not butted tightly, and the seaming tape shows.

Resolution: Builder should make the necessary repairs to meet the above Performance Guideline.

Recommendation: None. However, Homeowners should follow the flooring manufacturer's cleaning and care instructions.

CARPET IS LOOSE

Carpets should be stretched tightly, without areas of looseness. If the carpet is loose, the Builder should have it re-stretched.

Resolution: Builder should make the necessary repairs.

Recommendation: None. However, Homeowners should follow the flooring manufacturer's cleaning and care instructions.

CARPET FIBERS SEPARATE FROM BACKING

Carpet fibers usually do not separate from backing unless the carpet has been cleaned with improper products or has been allowed to remain wet for an extended period of time. Proper carpet maintenance is a Homeowner's Responsibility.

Resolution: Builder should deliver the finish floor in conformance with the above guidelines.

Recommendation: Do not clean carpet with improper products or allow it to remain wet for extended periods of time. Promptly clean any spills in accordance with the material manufacturer's recommendations.

FADING AND DISCOLORATION

Proper carpet maintenance is a Homeowner responsibility. Some amount of fading is unavoidable in areas that are exposed to sunlight. Spots are usually the result of spills or pet accidents. The Homeowner should promptly neutralize and remove any spills in a manner consistent with the manufacturer's recommendations.

Resolution: There should be no fades or discolorations at the time of the Walkthrough.

Recommendation: Choose carpet colors and types that will provide the longest life at sun-exposed locations. Do not let sunlight continuously beam onto carpet, as it may cause fading. Promptly clean any spills in accordance with the material manufacturer's recommendations.

PADDING MISSING UNDER PORTION OF THE CARPET

Carpet padding that is missing is unacceptable and should be added by the Builder. The exception to this is that some Builders choose to eliminate padding from closets that are not walk-in closets. This condition is acceptable in those areas.

Resolution: Builder should make the necessary repairs to meet the above guideline.

Recommendation: Homeowners should follow the manufacturer's cleaning and care instructions.

CARPET TEXTURE DOES NOT ALIGN AT SEAMS

Texture at seams should run in the same direction. Quarter turns are not acceptable.

Resolution: Builder should make the necessary repairs to meet the above Performance Guideline.

Recommendation: None. However, should follow the manufacturer's care and cleaning instructions.

CARPETS HAVE A DARK SOIL LINE AT STAIR AND BASEBOARD EDGES

Soil staining of carpets due to air infiltration can be reduced, but not eliminated at stair and baseboard edges. Builder should seal the plate behind the baseboard and stair edges with foam, caulk, or by making the joints tight.

Resolution: There should be no soil lines visible at the time of the Walkthrough.

Recommendation: Homeowner can expect some soiling to occur at baseboard and stair edges, even if the Builder has made a good faith effort to seal the edges. Homeowner should consider this when selecting carpet colors. Light colors can show edge marks in a short period of time.

THERE IS A BUMP AT THE TRANSITION BETWEEN CARPET AND HARD SURFACE FLOORING

There should be no more than 1/4-inch vertical displacement between different finish flooring surfaces. Ramping or floating the subfloor is an acceptable method to meet the Performance Guideline. Ramps should extend under the carpet at the rate of one foot horizontal for every 1/4-inch of vertical. Specifically designed transition strips, such as metal or wood, may be placed at the transition threshold to alert persons that they are stepping onto a different surface at a different level.

Resolution: Builder should perform appropriate repairs to satisfy the Guideline.

Recommendation: None.

COUNTERTOPS

COUNTERTOP IS NOT LEVEL

Countertops should not exceed 1/4-inch of rise or drop in any 8-foot direction. Exception: certain tiles are made with an intentionally irregular, lumpy surface and these irregularities are acceptable.

Resolution: Builder should take corrective actions to level the countertop, including leveling the cabinets, if necessary.

Recommendation: None.

BACKSLASH IS LOOSE

Countertop backslashes should be tightly adhered to the wall

Resolution: Builder should make the corrections to repair the loose backsplash.

Recommendation: Cabinets expand and shrink with room moisture. Cracks will occur between the top and the splash. Homeowner should maintain the cracks with caulk or grout.

CERAMIC TILE COUNTERTOPS

UNEVEN SURFACE

Since there are a number of different types of ceramic tile, ranging from rough handmade varieties to the very precisely manufactured types, it is impractical to apply any one standard to all ceramic tiles. The general guideline for an entire countertop is no more than 1/8-inch of uneven surface in any direction in eight feet horizontally. For handmade tiles, the condition is established by using a long straightedge that rests on multiple high points along the countertop length. For very regular manufactured tiles, in addition to the level guideline, no point should occur more than 1/16-inch above or below a line parallel to the surface, and adjacent tiles should not be more than 1/32-inch out of level with each other. Countertops can be totally level but should never slow away from drainage points such as sinks or basins.

Resolution: Builder should make repairs as necessary.

Recommendation: Always follow the manufacturer's care and cleaning recommendations for the specific ceramic tile.

UNEQUAL GROUT JOINTS

Different types of tiles call for grout joints of different widths. However, within any one area of tile (for precise and manufactured tiles), joints should not vary more than 1/32-inch from the widest to the narrowest.

Resolution: Builder should make repairs as necessary.

Recommendation: Always follow the manufacturer's care and cleaning recommendations for the specific ceramic tile

GROUT JOINT CRACKS

Hairline cracks may appear in grout joints where there are changes in the plane of the tile surface and where tile abuts a dissimilar material, such as at a backsplash or at a sink or wall. Excluding joints at changes in plane, cracks exceeding 5% of the total length of grout joint in any one-tile installation are considered non-performing.

Resolution: Builder should make repairs as necessary, provided the condition is not a result of inadequate Homeowner maintenance or misuse.

Recommendation: Homeowner should maintain caulking and repair incidental grout cracking, especially at backsplash and sink openings.

CRACKED TILE

Where cracks align across a number of consecutive tiles, the usual cause is movement of underlying building components. Isolated cracks in individual tiles may indicate Homeowner abuse of the countertop.

Resolution: If an underlying problem is identified after investigation, the Builder should make repairs as necessary.

Recommendation: Do not place unusually heavy objects on the tile surface; avoid dropping things on the tiles. Always follow the manufacturer's care and cleaning recommendations for the specific ceramic tile.

COLOR AND TEXTURE VARIATIONS

Tile used in any one area should be from the same batch, or lot, providing consistent appearance throughout. This does not apply to certain types of handmade tile in which variations are a desirable characteristic. Obvious changes in color and texture within a field of tile are not acceptable where the tile is intended to be of consistent appearance.

Resolution: Builder should make repairs as necessary.

Recommendation: Always follow the manufacturer's care and cleaning recommendations for the specific ceramic tile.

LOOSE TILE

Generally, tile should not come loose from the underlying surface to which it is applied. More specifically, tile can come loose as a result of improper original application of mortar, excessive deflection of the underlying material to which tile is applied or because of exposure to impact from heavy objects.

Resolution: If condition is a result of improper installation or construction and not a result of Homeowner misuse, Builder should make repairs as necessary.

Recommendation: Avoid dropping heavy objects on the tile surface. Always follow the manufacturer's care and cleaning recommendations for the specific ceramic tile.

WATER PENETRATION THROUGH TOP

Properly installed, countertops intended for use that involves exposure to significant amounts of water (food preparation areas, countertops adjacent to sinks and basins, etc.) should include a water resisting system adequate to prevent leaks through the countertop assembly.

Resolution: Builder should make repairs as necessary.

Recommendation: Always follow the manufacturer's care and cleaning recommendations for the specific ceramic tile

GRANITE, MARBLE, STONE COUNTERTOPS

CRACKS

Cracks in excess of 1/32-inch are considered non-performing. Cracks may be related to improper or inadequate installation, or a result of inadequate support. Improper use may also be a cause

Resolution: After investigation, Builder should repair or replace non-performing countertops as necessary; if the condition was not a result of improper use. Specialists in stone restoration should repair cracked marble, but before undertaking such repairs, the Builder should correct any underlying causes.

Recommendation: Maintain countertop in accordance with the recommendations of the material manufacturer and supplier. Maintain caulking and repair incidental grout cracking, especially at backsplash and sink openings. Do not drop heavy objects on countertops. Do not stand on countertop.

TEXTURE AND COLOR VARIATIONS

Countertops made up of multiple pieces should be assembled with reasonably well-matched colors. Severe variations in surface texture and color are unacceptable.

Resolution: Guideline should be met at the time of Home delivery.

Recommendation: While both texture and color are truly subjective in nature, a good rule of thumb is: If the Homeowner buys the House before the finish surfaces are set, the Homeowner should approve their placement. If the Homeowner buys the House after the finish surfaces are installed, the Homeowner accepts the finishes as installed.

STAINS

Granite marble and stone can be stained by a variety of products and natural materials, juices, etc. Protection of the surface is a Homeowner Responsibility. Any pre-existing stains should be noted at the time of the Homeowner Walkthrough.

Resolution: Builder should correct any pre-existing stains noted at the Walkthrough. If pre-existing stains cannot be corrected, Builder should replace countertop.

Recommendation: Examine countertops carefully at the Walkthrough. Builders cannot be held responsible for this type of damage unless it is identified and disclosed at the time of the Walkthrough. Maintain countertop in accordance with the recommendations of the material manufacturer and supplier. Use only cleaning products approved by the manufacturer or the applicable trade association for the material. Do not use abrasives to clean any type of countertop. Avoid placing hot pots, pans, Crockpots, etc. in direct contact with the countertop.

CHIPS

Granite, marble, and stone countertops should not be delivered to the Homeowner scratched or chipped. Repairs of chips and scratches prior to the Walkthrough are acceptable provided the repair cannot be distinguished at a distance of six feet under normal lighting conditions. Chips on a top of any material should not penetrate more than 1/16-inch from the edge of the seam or grout joint, unless the manufacturing process intentionally created edge chips.

Resolution: Repair or replace countertops as necessary, provided that condition was not caused by Homeowner misuse or negligence.

Recommendation: Examine countertops carefully at the Walkthrough. Maintain countertop in accordance with the recommendations of the material manufacturer and supplier. Do not drop heavy objects on countertop.

PLASTIC LAMINATE COUNTERTOPS

OPEN JOINTS

A properly assembled plastic laminate countertop should have tight hairline joints without any openings where adjoining pieces meet. Joints that are separated by more than 1/32-inch are considered unacceptable and should be corrected by the Builder.

Resolution: Builder should repair or replace countertops as necessary, provided that condition was not caused by Homeowner misuse or negligence.

Recommendation: Examine countertops carefully at the Walkthrough. Maintain countertop in accordance with the recommendations of the material manufacturer and supplier.

DELAMINATION

Delamination occurs when the plastic laminate does not adhere to the underlayment. This is usually an adhesive application problem or curing problem. Edge strips are most commonly affected by this type of problem. Delamination is unacceptable and should be corrected by the Builder unless there is evidence of abusive use by the Homeowner.

Resolution: Builder should repair or replace countertops as necessary, provided that the condition was not caused by Homeowner misuse or negligence.

Recommendation: Maintain countertop in accordance with the recommendations of the material manufacturer and supplier. Maintain caulking, especially at backsplash and sink openings.

UNACCEPTABLE TRIMMING

Unacceptable trimming can include edges that are not straight and edges that are burned because of overheating of trimming cutters. Trimmed edges should be very straight and neat. The edge exposure area should be of a constant width throughout the countertop.

Resolution: Builder should repair or replace countertops as necessary.

Recommendation: Homeowner should maintain countertop in accordance with the recommendations of the material manufacturer and supplier.

STAINS AND BURNS

The countertop should be delivered to the Homeowner without stains, scratches, or burns.

Resolution: Builder should repair or replace any non-performing conditions noted at the time of the Walkthrough.

Recommendation: Examine countertops carefully at the Walkthrough. Builders cannot be held responsible for this type of damage unless it is identified and disclosed at the time of the Walkthrough. Maintain countertop in accordance with the recommendations of the material manufacturer and supplier. Use only cleaning products approved by the material manufacturer, never use abrasives. Avoid placing hot objects on countertops.

SOLID SURFACE COUNTERTOPS

OPEN SEAMS

Depending on the selected color and veining, there should be no conspicuous seams in the finished countertop. Proficient solid surface countertop installers are able to bond adjacent pieces so that the joint is virtually inconspicuous, but not necessarily invisible. Some solid surface pieces may be "soft-seamed" with a flexible silicone.

Resolution: Builder should repair or replace countertops as necessary.

Recommendation: Homeowner should examine countertops carefully at the Walkthrough. Maintain countertop in accordance with the recommendations of the material manufacturer and supplier.

ROUGHENED SURFACE

To finish solid surface countertops, it is necessary to sand the surface smooth. The resulting final surface should be smooth and consistent throughout. Surface texture variations that are clearly rough to the touch are considered unacceptable.

Resolution: Builder should repair or replace countertops as necessary, provided that condition was not caused by Homeowner misuse or negligence.

Recommendation: Homeowner should examine countertops carefully at the Walkthrough. Maintain countertop in accordance with the recommendations of the material manufacturer and supplier.

STAINS AND BURNS

There should be no stains or burns on any portion of the countertop at the time of the Homeowner Walkthrough.

Resolution: Builder should repair or replace any non-performing conditions noted at the Walkthrough.

Recommendation: Examine countertops carefully at the Walkthrough. Maintain countertop in accordance with the recommendations of the material manufacturer and supplier. Builders cannot be held responsible for this type of damage unless it is identified and disclosed at the time of the Walkthrough.

BLEMISHES AND SCRATCHES

A solid surface countertop is a product that is manufactured under closely controlled conditions. Therefore the countertop should be delivered to the Homeowner free of blemishes and scratches.

Resolution: Builder should repair or replace countertops as necessary.

Recommendation: Homeowner should examine countertops carefully at the Walkthrough. Maintain countertop in accordance with the recommendations of the material manufacturer and supplier. Builders cannot be held responsible for this type of damage unless it is identified and disclosed at the time of the Walkthrough.

CULTURE MARBLE COUNTERTOPS

The top and backsplash pieces should fit together without gaps. The installer is likely to caulk these joints with a compatible caulk. If there is a gap between the backsplash and the wall, this gap should also be caulked so that no gap is visible. No gap should be more than 1/4-inch wide, whether caulked or not.

Resolution: Builder should repair or replace countertops as necessary.

Recommendation: Examine countertops carefully at the Walkthrough. Maintain countertop in accordance with the recommendation of the material manufacturer and supplier.

BLEMISHES AND INCONSISTENT COLOR

Color swirls can vary significantly in cultured marble due to the fact that each batch is made like a marble cake. In general, the color swirls should be consistent throughout the top, and should not be concentrated in any one spot. The same guideline applies to any sparkles, if added to the mix.

Resolution: Builder shall repair or replace countertops as necessary.

Recommendation: Examine countertops carefully at the Walkthrough. Maintain countertop in accordance with the recommendation of the material manufacturer and supplier.

VOIDS AT SURFACE

There should be no voids (depressions) in the surface more than 1/32-inch in depth and no larger than one inch in diameter. There should be no more than four such voids in 8 square feet of surface.

Resolution: Repair or replace countertops as necessary, provided that condition was not caused by Homeowner misuse or negligence.

Recommendation: Examine countertops carefully at the Walkthrough. Maintain countertop in accordance with the recommendations of the material manufacturer and supplier. Do not drop heavy objects on countertop surfaces.

LEAKS AT JOINTS AND FITTINGS

All penetrations at the facets sink rims and back splashes should be watertight.

Resolution: Builder shall repair any unacceptable conditions.

Recommendation: Always maintain the countertop in accordance with the manufacturer's recommendations. If at any time Homeowner discovers product or installation problems, the Homeowner should notify the Builder promptly.

APPLIANCES

APPLIANCES DO NOT PERFORM AS INTENDED

All appliances should function in the manner that the manufacturer intended.

Resolution: Builder should repair the appliance in a prompt manner in accordance with the manufacturer's warranty.

Recommendation: Register all appliances with the manufacturer. Read and follow the manufacturer's operation instructions. Before making a service call, follow the Trouble Shooting Guide found in the appliance owner's manuals.

CABINETS AND VANITIES

CABINETS DESIGNED TO SET FLUSH WITH THE CEILING HAVE A VISIBLE GAP, SPACE, OR SEPARATION

Any space or gap along the top or sides of the cabinet frame that exceeds 3/16-inch is considered unacceptable.

Resolution: All cabinets should have the proper backing in the wall to support whatever product is being applied to that particular wall. If the cabinet or vanity does not meet the guideline and was not a result of negligence by the Homeowner, then the Builder should repair as necessary.

Recommendation: Homeowner should use caution when loading upper cabinets so as to not overload them. Heavy plates and dishes and canned goods do not belong in upper cabinets.

CABINETS ARE NOT SET *FLUSH* WITH ONE ANOTHER

The face (front) of a cabinet should not be more than 1/8 inch out of flat plane with connecting portions of other cabinet pieces. Corners should not be out of line more than 3/16 inches.

Resolution: If the cabinets do not meet the above Performance Guideline, then the Builder should repair or replace any non-performing cabinetry in order to satisfy the Guideline. When finishing or refinishing, Builder should attempt to match the original cabinetry.

Recommendation: The Homeowner should properly maintain all cabinets, particularly any cabinetry that is located in areas that are subject to moisture, i.e. kitchens, bathrooms or laundry rooms. Water should not be allowed to remain on any wood products, whether sealed or not. If it is determined that the Homeowner was negligent with maintenance, the Builder will not be held responsible.

CABINETS ARE WARPED

Cabinet doors should not warp more than ¼ inch from the face of the frame. If the door is flat, but the frame is warped, the same Performance Guideline applies.

Resolution: Any cabinet or cabinetry, including doors and drawer fronts, that do not meet the above Performance Guideline should be replaced either in part or in whole (assuming condition was not cause by Homeowner negligence). When finishing or refinishing, Builder should attempt to match the original cabinetry.

Recommendation: Cabinets, drawer fronts and doors need to be periodically inspected for excessive wear and/or deterioration of the finish.

CABINET DRAWER GUIDE HAS BROKEN

All doors and drawers should function smoothly and properly for their intended purpose.

Resolution: If a drawer or door does not meet the above guideline, then the Builder should repair or replace the portion of the cabinet that does not conform.

Recommendation: Homeowner should be careful not to overload the drawers. This puts additional stress on the guides, which could cause them to prematurely fail.

CABINET DRAWER IS BINDING DURING OPENING

Cabinet doors and drawers should open and close smoothly without tugging or pulling

Resolution: Builder should repair or replace the drawer or door that does not perform.

Recommendation: Homeowner should operate doors and drawers smoothly and easily. Do not overload the drawers. Metal drawer guides should be lubricated with light lubricating oil every two years.

CABINET DOOR SWING OPEN AND / OR WILL NOT STAY CLOSED

All door hinge mechanisms and catches should operate and function as intended. Whether closing or opening, the door should operate smoothly with reasonable ease or effort.

Resolution: Builder should repair or replace the drawer or door that does not meet the guideline.

Recommendation: Doors can go out of adjustment, depending upon the care and use that they have been put through. Do not slam, hang objects from, or pull on the door, as this will cause hinge mechanisms to weaken not only at their fastening points but also within the mechanisms themselves. Periodically inspect hinges and retighten if necessary.

DOORS OR DRAWERS HAVE CRACKS IN THE PANELS

Panel inserts in drawers and doors should not crack.

Resolution: Builder should replace cracked panels. An exact match of the wood grain or color cannot be expected.

Recommendation: Consider stained cabinets as furniture and treat the wood faces with furniture polish.

PLASTIC LAMINATE SURFACES ARE PEELING AWAY

Cabinets that are covered with high-pressure plastic laminate should not delaminate.

Resolution: If the cabinet delaminates and is not a result of negligence by the Homeowner, the Builder should make the repairs as necessary.

Recommendation: Proper care by the Homeowner is essential. Liquids should be cleaned up immediately and not left on a surface, particularly at joints or corners. This creates the potential for the breakdown of the glues used to laminate the surface to the substrate.

CABINETS DO NOT SIT LEVEL

Cabinets should not have a deviation of more than 3/8-inch out of level over 6 feet of length.

Resolution: Builder should make repairs as necessary. When finishing or refinishing, Builder should attempt to match the original cabinetry.

Recommendation: None.

CABINET DOORS DO NOT ALIGN WHEN CLOSED

Gaps between abutting doors should not exceed 1/8-inch.

Resolution: Builder should adjust doors to meet the guideline.

Recommendation: None.

CABINET FINISH (PAINT OR STAIN) IS IRREGULAR, MISMATCHED, OR BLOTCHY

Irregularities of wood color in stained cabinets are considered acceptable, unless two or more different stains were used. Painted cabinets should be uniform in color when viewed under normal lighting conditions at a distance of 6 feet.

Resolution: Builder should take corrective action to meet the above performance guideline.

Recommendation: None.

GAPS APPEAR BETWEEN SECTIONS WHERE CABINETS ARE JOINED

Gaps at the section where cabinet cases are joined that are in excess of 1/32-inch for painted cabinets and 1/16-inch for stained cabinets are considered unacceptable

Resolution: Builder should make repairs as necessary.

Recommendation: Be aware that painted cabinets will separate at the stiles due to normal drying out of the house frame. Bathroom and laundry fans should always be operating when those rooms are in use.

STAIN GRADE CABINETS SHOW A "DARK" BAND AROUND DOOR AND DRAWER OPENINGS

This condition can occur from the sun fading exposed areas of cabinetry.

Resolution: None.

Recommendation: If the Homeowner wants to achieve a uniform color, they can leave the doors and drawers slightly open and exposed to the light. This procedure may take up to a year to achieve a uniform result.

MIRRORS

SCRATCHES ON GLASS SURFACE

If scratches or imperfections are visible under normal lighting conditions and are noticeable from a distance of 3 feet or more, the mirror is considered non-performing (providing the glass was not damaged as a result of any Homeowner negligence).

Resolution: If the mirror does not meet the guideline, then the Builder should replace the mirror.

Recommendation: The Homeowner should thoroughly inspect all mirrors for any irregularities within the glazing at the time of the Walkthrough.

MIRROR BACKING IS DETERIORATING

When viewing the mirror from the front, there should be no visible imperfections, peeling, flaking and/or discoloration within the metallic backing material of the mirror.

Resolution: Builder should replace any mirror that does not conform to the guideline.

Recommendation: Homeowner should thoroughly inspect all mirrors for any irregularities within the glazing and its metallic backing at the time of the walkthrough. When cleaning a mirror, use caution when using cleaners that contain ammonia or vinegar. Ammonia and vinegar are excellent glass cleaners, however they can be extremely damaging to the metallic backing of the mirror. Also, do not allow cleaners to go over the top, sides or to get into the track at the bottom of the mirror. Manufacturers often recommended applying cleaning agents to a cloth, and then wiping down the mirror.

MIRROR WARDROBE DOORS DO NOT HAVE SAFETY BACKING (WALK-IN CLOSETS)

Mirror wardrobe doors used as the entry to walk-in closets should have safety backing with labels stating that they have met the following standards: ANSI Z97

Resolution: Builder should replace all mirror doors used on walk-in closets and do not meet this standard.

Recommendation: None.

SHOWER AND TUB ENCLOSURES

GLASS/PLASTIC IS SCRATCHED

At the time of delivery of the House, shower and tub enclosure glass or plastic panels should not be scratched.

Resolution: Builder should replace any glass or plastic panels that are scratched at the time of the Walkthrough.

Recommendation: Be aware that any claims for scratched shower and tub enclosure panels may not be honored by the Builder after the walkthrough.

SHOWER OR TUB ENCLOSURES LEAK

Shower doors should not leak through the frame. Shower enclosures should not leak through the joint between the door edge and the frame, or at the door bottom.

Resolution: Builder should make necessary repairs so there is no leakage at the enclosures frame (this excludes the intersection of the two movable panels on a tub enclosure). If there is leakage at the shower enclosure door, determine if it is improper installation or Homeowner caused by directing the showerhead at the door opening while showering.

Recommendation: Become aware of the proper use of a tub and shower enclosure. Keep shower water directed away from the door and panels. Continuous leaking may result in rot of the underlayment and subfloor. Continuous leaking also creates an environment for mold and mildew growth and for termites. The enclosure track should never be used as a handle to pull a bather up into a standing position.

FIBERGLASS OR ACRYLIC TUB BOTTOM OR SHOWER STALL ENCLOSURE FLEXES WHEN OCCUPIED

Some flexing of tub and shower sidewalls and bases is permissible, as long as the installation conforms to the manufacturer's guidelines.

Resolution: If the tub or shower has been installed in accordance with the manufacturer's instructions, the Builder does not have any responsibility. If the tub or shower has not been installed per the manufacturer's installation instructions, Builder shall make necessary repairs to conform the manufacturer's instructions.

Recommendation: Homeowner has a duty to learn the care and maintenance of synthetic bath surfaces, and shall notify Builder if the fitting cracks or pulls away from its supports.

SHOWER/TUB ENCLOSURES ARE NOT TEMPERED GLASS

If glass is used in shower and tub enclosures, it must be tempered. If plastic panels are used, they must be approved by the local Building Official.

Resolution: Unless approved plastic is used in shower and tub enclosures, all glass panels should be tempered.

Recommendation: None.

TOP RAIL OF SHOWER/TUB ENCLOSURE IS NOT SCREWED TO THE FRAME

The top rail of a tub or shower enclosure should be screwed to the frame or mechanically connected in a manner approved by the local Building Official.

Resolution: The Builder should take the necessary corrective measures to conform to the above requirement.

Recommendation: None.

GROUT IS CRACKED BETWEEN THE TUB/SHOWER AND FIRST ROW OF TILE

The grout should not be cracked at the bottom of the first course of tile at the time of Walkthrough (hairline cracks are expected.)

Resolution: Builder shall make repairs as necessary if grout cracks are noted at Walkthrough.

Recommendation: Tile grout should be sealed by the Homeowner prior to use; with a silicone-based sealer that can be purchased at any hardware store. Grout should be cleaned frequently and should be kept free of mold and mildew. When significant cracking first appears, the gout joint between the bottom row of tile and the top of the shower floor or tub should be caulked with a caulking compound made for bathroom use. Many grout manufacturers also make flexible sealants, both standard and smooth, to match their grout colors. Old caulk or grout should be dug out and discarded; new caulk should not be applied over old caulk.

WATER RESISTANT BACKING IMPROPERLY INSTALLED AT TUB OR SHOWER SURROUNDINGS

If backing is to be used at tub and shower surrounds, it must be water-resistant. Materials such as cement board or special water resistant paper may be used. However, lath and mortar are preferred. Water-resistant gypsum board is a Code-permitted alternative.

Resolution: Builder should use an appropriate water-resistant backing material at tub and shower surrounds and water-resistant drywall at other potentially damps locations.

Recommendation: Make certain that a coat of premium enamel paint is maintained on the drywall surface in. Maintain the caulking between the tubs or shower pan and the first row of tile.

ELECTRICAL

LIGHTS FLICKER WHEN APPLIANCES ARE TURNED ON

If the circuit is not overloaded by the Homeowner, and if lightly flicker continuously and the breaker do not trip, the circuit is unacceptable.

Resolution: The Builder should inspect the circuit, determine the problem, and make the necessary repairs. The Builder is not responsible for momentary flickering when high capacity appliances are plugged into wall outlets.

Recommendation: Avoid overloading circuits with multiple appliances and add-on outlets. If wires feel warm to the touch, they should be unplugged and reinserted into a separate circuit. Note: Circuit breakers are found in the main panel where the meter is located or in the subpanel. The circuits should be labeled inside the panels.

BREAKERS TRIP OR FUSES BLOW FREQUENCY

Circuit breakers that trip frequently and fuses that blow frequently, under proper design usage, are indications of an unacceptable circuit or a malfunctioning appliance.

Resolution: Builder should test circuits to determine their capacity and make necessary corrections if the circuits are found to be inadequate for expected normal usage by the Homeowner.

Recommendation: Homeowner should not overload circuits to the point where fuses blow or breakers trip. If frequent tripping occurs, the Homeowner has a duty to notify the Builder. **DO NOT replace a fuse or circuit breaker with one that has a higher rating or one made by a different manufacturer! This action could result in a fire.**

GROUND FAULT INTERRUPTER TRIPS FREQUENTLY

Ground fault interrupters should be installed in accordance with the National Electric Code or other applicable Code in effect at the time.

Resolution: None, assuming the installation was done pursuant to the applicable Code and that the GFI device itself is acceptable.

Recommendation: Test GFIs monthly by pressing the black test button. Do not plug a freezer or refrigerator into a GFI outlet.

ALUMINUM WIRE, NOT COPPER WIRE, WAS INSTALLED

House wiring should be installed per applicable Code.

Resolution: Builder should install wiring per applicable Code.

Recommendation: None.

LIGHT FIXTURES TARNISH

Light fixtures should not be tarnished at time of delivery of House.

Resolution: Builder shall repair or replace fixtures that do not conform at time of delivery of the House.

Recommendation: Inspect fixtures during the Walkthrough. Check with fixture manufacturers regarding their warranty. Fixtures, especially bright brass, will need to be cleaned and polished as routine maintenance.

LIGHT SWITCHES AND OUTLET PLATES PROTRUDE TOO FAR FROM WALL

Switch and plug plates that protrude more than 1/16-inch from the finished wall are considered unacceptable.

Resolution: Builder should adjust switch and outlet plates to be flush and level in the wall. For minor protrusions less than 1/16-inch, caulking in an acceptable repair.

Recommendation: None.

LIGHT SWITCHES STICK OR MUST BE JIGGLED TO TURN THE LIGHT ON

Light switches that stick or require tapping or jiggling to turn on lights or appliance are unacceptable.

Resolution: Builder should replace all light switches that operate in a non-performing manner

Recommendation: None.

WALL OUTLET IN BEDROOM DOES NOT WORK

A bedroom must have an overhead light or a wall outlet that is turned on from a switch by the door.

Resolution: None, assuming that the outlet is properly switched.

Recommendation: The wall outlet (also known as a "half hot", and is typically installed upside down to identify it) is controlled by the light switch. Flip the light switch on and the outlet should operate.

BATHROOM FANS / LAUNDRY FANS ARE NOISY

These fans can be noisy. This is not a condition of non-performance unless the sound is a result of fan blades hitting part of the housing unit.

Resolution: Unless the fan blades are hitting the housing or other solid object, Builder has no responsibility.

Recommendation: Do not disconnect the bath or laundry fans because they create an annoying noise. Moist air must be exhausted to the outside; otherwise mold and mildew can form on the walls and ceiling. Fans should be operated while these rooms are in use.

PLUMBING

WATER OR GAS PIPING LEAKS

Water supply piping, gas piping, wastewater piping, and fire sprinkler plumbing should not leak. Piping must contain and convey 100% of the liquid or gas that it is intended to convey.

Resolution: Builder should make corrective repairs to any leaking piping system. Builder is not responsible for piping leaks caused by earthquakes or shifts in the structure that were not caused by Builder.

Recommendation: The Homeowner has a duty to notify the Builder upon noticing any gas or liquid leaks in piping, no matter how small. Failure to give timely notice can result in health hazards, personal injury, and structural damage, etc. Homeowner should have the fire sprinkler system professionally tested annually (or more frequently if required by the local fire authorities) to determine that the system will operate as designed in the event of a fire.

WATER PIPES FREEZE

In geographic areas where freezing weather is normal, water supply and waste piping should be protected from freezing. For geographic areas where freezing weather is rare, unprotected pipes are considered acceptable.

Resolution: Protect all pipes from freezing weather if the House is constructed in an areas where freezing weather is normal and customary. If the Homeowner does not maintain minimum heat, the Builder is not responsible for any leaking pipes due to freezing that occurs in any portion of the House that is intended to be heated.

Recommendation: To protect against the nuisance of infrequent freezing weather, the Homeowner can at his or her option purchase protective materials such as pipe insulation and electric resistant heat tape at any local hardware store. If the Homeowner is going to be gone for a period of time during possible freezing weather, the thermostat should be set on "heat" at its minimum setting.

WATER TASTES FUNNY, SMELLS, OR IS DISCOLORED

Water should be of good quality. However, the Builder may not have control over the quality of water supplied by the local water district.

Resolution: None, unless the Builder is responsible for creating the water supply to the house. This does not mean installing the water piping system that is to be taken over by a municipal authority. If the Builder is responsible for supplying the source of water, the Builder, should provide water that meets minimum quality standards as set by the governing agency, such as the local County Department of Health or the State of California Department of Water Quality. The Builder should not be responsible for changes in water quality once the quality meets the local or State set standards. For example, a change in nearby agricultural uses, or mining activity subsequent to construction, may cause changes in water quality that are not the Builders Responsibility.

Recommendation: If water quality standards are met by the Builder and/or the local water supply agency, and are still unacceptable to the

Homeowner, consider a whole house filtration system or use of a drinking water service company.

TOLIET BACKS UP, DRAINS BACK UP

At the time of the Walkthrough, all fixtures should operate as intended and all drains should flow freely.

Resolution: Builder is not responsible for post-Walkthrough conditions, unless it can be determined that the cause of the blockage was from construction related activity.

Recommendation: Sink, tub, and shower traps should be kept free and clear as routine maintenance items. Material such as hair, toothpaste, sanitary napkins, etc. may accumulate in the traps and could eventually cause a backup. Try to keep these materials from getting into the trap in the first place, and use a drain cleaner every 3-4 months to keep the traps scoured out and free from debris build-up. Learn the proper use of a low-flush toilet.

INADEQUATE WATER PRESSURE

For Houses that are connected to the municipal water system or mutual water system of 10 houses or more, the House piping system should be designed to operate between pressures of 15psi and 80psi. For Houses that are connected to a well or a mutual water system of 10 houses or fewer, the water pressure should be subject to the capacity of the well and the output of its equipment.

Resolution: Provided the Builder has met the local Code for water pipe system sizing, the Builder has no responsibility.

Recommendation: In areas where the water service is at the lower end of the allowable pressure range, water flows from fixtures will be less. This condition is beyond the control of the Builder and should be addressed with the agency that supplies that water. If the problem persists, consider installing a booster pump to increase pressure. Using several fixtures simultaneously may also result in low water flow and decrease in pressure.

SEWER GAS SMELL COMING FROM DRAIN

This is a Homeowner maintenance item unless the sewer gas is coming from a cracked pipe

Resolution: None.

Recommendation: Sewer gas smells coming from drains typically indicate a lack of water in the trap. This occurs when a drain is not used for long periods of time and the water evaporates from the trap. Pouring a large glass of water in the drain will fill the trap sufficiently.

COPPER WATER PIPES OR BLACK GAS PIPES ARE WET ON THE OUTSIDE

Condensation on the outside of water lines is normal condition

Resolution: Builder should install pipe insulation on cold water pipes where there is a likelihood of condensation and mold growth.

Recommendation: None.

FAUCETS DRIP

At the time of the Walkthrough, all washers and cartridges should seat tightly and faucets should not leak.

Resolution: Any faucets that leak at the time of the Walkthrough should be repaired.

Recommendation: Washers and cartridges should be replaced at the time when dripping is first noticed. Many cartridges have a 5-year to lifetime guarantee on parts. Most of the current bathroom and kitchen faucets are made with cartridges and require only infrequent replacement. Hose bibs (the valves that a hose is connected to on the outside of the House) are made with washers. Depending upon the amount of use, hose bib washers may need to be replaced as frequently as every six months or as infrequently as every 3 years. If leaking occurs at the "stem" or handle of the valve (often at the hose bib or water heater), the nut at the base of the stem can be tightened or repacked to solve this problem.

SINK/TUB IS CHIPPED

Fixtures should not be chipped at time of delivery. Chips, mars, or discolorations 1/32-inch or less are considered acceptable

Resolution: Builder shall repair any chips, mars, or discolorations that exceed the above standard that are observed at the time of the Walkthrough.

Recommendation: None.

SHOWER HEAD PIPE/TUB SPOUT IS LOOSE

At time of delivery, showerhead pipes and tub spouts should be secured so they cannot move in or out more than 1/4-inch

Resolution: Non-conforming conditions shall be cured when noted at time of the Walkthrough.

Recommendation: Avoid hanging heavy objects such as shower caddies full of bating shampoos and lotions on the showerhead pipe.

FIBERGLASS TUB/SHOWER FLEXES WHEN OCCUPIED

Fiberglass and acrylic tub and shower units should be installed in accordance with the manufacturer's instructions.

Resolution: If installation is not made in accordance with the manufacturer's instructions, Builder should correct the non-performing condition.

Recommendation: None.

WATER DRAINS FROM SINK/TUB WHEN STOPPED IS ENGAGED

Water should not drain past the stopper mechanism at a rate of which the depth of water in the sink or tub decreases by more than one-inch per hour.

Resolution: Sinks and tubs which drain more quickly than permitted under the guideline, and whose stoppers have been properly maintained, should be adjusted or replaced as necessary.

Recommendation: Periodic cleaning and maintenance of mechanical sink and tub stoppers is a Homeowner responsibility. Stoppers should be checked monthly.

BRASS BATHROOM FAUCETS AND DRAINS TARNISH

Brass fittings should be free from tarnish at the time of delivery; brass fittings that become tarnished subsequent to the Walkthrough are acceptable.

Resolution: Builder shall replace any brass fittings on bathroom fixtures that are tarnished at the time of the Walkthrough.

Recommendation: Brass is beautiful but "soft" metal. It is easily scratched and tarnished. Follow the manufacturer's instructions when cleaning brass. Cleansers with abrasives and cleansers with ammonia are likely to scratch and chemically attack brass finishes. Wipe brass finishes frequently.

TOLIET RUNS CONTINUOUSLY

When a toilet tank fills, it should shut off. Water should not run continuously through the overflow pipe or flapper valve.

Resolution: Builder should make corrections to toilet tank system so that the water shuts off when the tank is filled to the appropriate level.

Recommendation: Toilet tanks have mechanical parts inside them and these parts wear out over time. Depending upon the amount of use and water quality, replacing worn flappers, floats, and valves can occur as frequently as once a year or as infrequently as every 10 years. Water supplies with higher concentrations of minerals (known as hard water) will leave deposits inside the toilet tank and its parts. This condition will cause more frequent replacement and rebuilding of toilet parts than those areas that do not have high mineral content in the water supply.

TOLIET LEAKS AT FLOOR

Toilets should not leak at the floor

Resolution: Builder should make necessary repairs to ensure a watertight flow between the toilet and the House waste plumbing.

Recommendation: The Homeowner has the duty to notify the Builder of any leaking toilet before additional damage occurs. Toilets that are permitted to leak will cause structural damage if the toilet is located over a wood subfloor. A toilet that leaks creates a condition for termites to enter the House, regardless of whether it sits on a wooden subfloor or a slab. Termites are attracted to dark, damp conditions in the soil. It is important to note that a toilet that rocks back and forth or moves side to side may be leaking, even though no leak is visible. The Homeowner has a duty to notify the Builder of this condition.

LACK OF HOT WATER

Builder should provide a hot water system, either gas or electric, that supplies hot water to all appropriate fixtures in the House. Some Energy Codes do not require that all hot water pipes that pass through unheated spaces (such as garages, crawl spaces, and attics) should be insulated provided that the Builder has installed other energy conserving devices that make the entire House code complaint. See your local code requirement for specific requirements.

Resolution: If the above Standard is not met, Builder should take corrective measures so that it is met.

Recommendation: Frequent demand over short time periods (such as morning showers by an entire family) can result in a lack of hot water until the water heater has had time to recover; this is not a Builder responsibility. If the Homeowner wishes to increase water temperature, he or she can adjust the control dial on most water heaters. Electric water heaters are often pre-set and cannot be adjusted. However, it is very important to recognize that the higher the temperature setting, the greater the danger of scalding. **CAUTION!** Before entering the tub or shower, always turn on water and adjust it to a safe and proper temperature. Children, elderly people (or any person), should never be placed in a tub or shower before the water is turned on and the temperature safely adjusted. Although many of the gas water heaters today have automatic ignition systems, the Homeowner should become familiar with how to manually light a water heater pilot.

WATER HEATER IS NOT EARTHQUAKE SECURED, AS REQUIRED

Water heater should be strapped or secured in Code approved manner to prevent tip-over during an earthquake.

Resolution: If the water heater is not strapped or secured to the frame of the House in a manner prescribed by Code, Builder should take the proper corrective measures.

Recommendation: None.

ELECTRIC WATER HEATER CIRCUIT BREAKER TRIPS CONTINUOUSLY

Electric water heater breakers should not trip. Tripping is an indication of an electrical problem within the heater or the wiring to the heater.

Resolution: Builder should take corrective measures to eliminate electrical water heater breaker tripping.

Recommendation: As electric water heaters age, their heating element can wear out and fall to the bottom of the tank. If this condition occurs, the circuit breaker cannot be reset, and the Homeowner needs to replace the water heater.

MATERIAL CHARACTERISTICS AND MAINTENANCE GUIDELINES

All construction materials, appliances and equipment have projected life expectancy maximums and performance thresholds. The intensity of use and the timeliness and effectiveness of preventive maintenance directly affect all components. To help prolong the enjoyment and longevity of your new project, we offer these **MATERIAL CHARACTERISTICS AND MAINTENANCE GUIDELINES** as an effort to provide helpful maintenance information. In case of a contradiction in these guidelines, refer to the manufacturers' instructions and recommendations which take precedence.

These suggestions and guidelines are not all inclusive and you should remember the performance of the systems and materials will vary with each individual home. If a component in your home is not performing to your expectations after following the prescribed maintenance, please bring the situation to the attention of your Contractor for informational assistance or for directions in submitting a **Warranty Service Request,** if appropriate.

APPLIANCES

MATERIAL CHARACTERISTICS

Appliances are considered "consumer products" and are specifically covered by a Manufacturers' warranty. To activate your warranty and service, be sure to complete and mail in the warranty registration cards right after your installation.

Home appliances, such as your range, microwave and dishwasher come with an explanation of features, care and cleaning requirements and directions on how to obtain warranty service.

Your dishwasher will be installed with a water supply hookup. Should the dishwasher malfunction and cause a water leak, the water shutoff valve is located in the cabinet beneath the kitchen sink. It is possible the same supply valve used for the dishwasher controls the cold water supply for the kitchen sink.

Although water supply valves have been installed in the home for a refrigerator icemaker and washing machine, the Homeowner is responsible for the connection of the appliance(s) to the supply valve(s). After the connection has been made, turn the shutoff valve counter-clockwise to turn the water ON. These shutoff valves will be demonstrated to you by your Contractor. These valves are similar to the sink faucet valves.

The common rubber hoses on your washing machine tend to wear out over time, similar to a radiator hose on a car. A burst hose can cause a tremendous amount of water damage to the home, especially if the home happens to be unoccupied when the event occurs. It is advisable to invest in upgraded hoses with braided stainless steel jacketing (these types of hoses are also available for the icemaker connection). Regardless, consult with a plumber or your home improvements center as to the anticipated life span of your hose(s) and then replace them on the timetable even if they do not show signs of wearing out.

If a gas appliance has been installed in your home, the in-line shutoff valve should be demonstrated to you. If the appliance is leaking gas, turn the valve perpendicular to the line to the "OFF" position and ventilate the room. If you still smell a gas odor after turning OFF the in-line valve and ventilating the room, turn OFF the main supply to the house at the gas meter and call your local gas provider.

If a gas stub has been provided for supply to a clothes dryer. <u>Please note a shutoff valve has not been supplied or installed for connection to the clothes dryer.</u> The Homeowner is responsible for the connection of the appliance to the supply. An in-line shutoff should be installed directly onto the gas stub. The gas flex line can then be run from the shutoff to the appliance. Consult with your local Gas provider regarding the proper installation procedure.

MAINTENANCE GUIDELINES

1. Thoroughly read the owner's manual(s) supplied with your appliance(s). Although much of the information may seem like common sense, some points may differ significantly from previous products you have owned or operated. Always follow the operation and safety guidelines and requirements contained in the publication.
2. It is the homeowners' responsibility to see that the flex vent on their dryer is properly attached to the fixed vent provided in their home. It is recommended that this hook-up be done by a qualified appliance installer or plumber. Once installed, the homeowners should check the vent system regularly, both at the dryer unit and where the vent exits the home, to be certain that airflow is unobstructed and the vent is free of lint build-up.
3. Power assist fans to the dryer venting system are required by the building code in some plan types. If a dryer assist fan was installed in your new home, this unit will require periodic maintenance by a professional (heating and air contractor or electrician).
4. Never put lye or drain clearing chemicals into the dishwasher as they may cause permanent damage.
5. Do not use steel wool, abrasives, ammonia or commercial oven cleaners on metal parts of your appliances. To safely clean these surfaces, wash with a mild soap, rinse, and then dry with a soft cloth. Follow Manufacturer's cleaning recommendations.
6. Glass cleaner may be used for glass surfaces, and polish with a soft, dry cloth. Do not allow the water or cleaner to run down inside openings in the glass.

CABINETS

MATERIAL CHARACTERISTICS

The cabinetry in your home has a factory-applied finish. Only high quality hardwoods are used for the fabrication of the cabinets.

Because no two trees are alike, the lumber cut from the trees varies in color and in character markings, such as grain patterns and mineral marks. Some species of wood will even vary in color depending on the time of year it is harvested.

You may notice some variations in the appearance of your cabinets due to natural imperfections in the wood and inconsistencies in the wood grain. Variations in wood grain and color on stained wood cabinets doors, drawers, end panels, corn mold, filler panels and wood trim are inherent to natural wood surface which create the warmth and natural beauty of the finished product. The variations are normal and unavoidable, and are not considered defects.

If your cabinets have a stain finish, the stain is sealed at the factory with a clear acrylic coating. The finish may tend to turn yellow due to exposure to sunlight and/or heat generated by appliances in the kitchen. Also, as the cabinet's age, the hardwood may start to darken. Because of these normal material characteristics, any replacement parts cannot be guaranteed to match the existing cabinets.

Please note the stain on pre-finished cabinets might not match the stain on pre-finished wood floor, entry doors, stair rails, stair tread nosing, etc.

MAINTENANCE GUIDELINES

1. Clean and polish your wood cabinets as you do your fine wood furniture. For a cleaning solution use a mild solution of dishwashing soap and water. Dry completely and do not allow water or other liquids to remain on the surface. Apply furniture wax or oil for surface protection.
2. To clean painted, laminated or thermofoil surfaces, use only a mild soap with warm water. Do not use any cleaning product which contains an abrasive of any kind. Consult professional refinisher for scratches and/or gouges.
3. **Note:** If repairs or replacements are scheduled, please do not clean or polish the affected surfaces until the defects are corrected.

COUNTERTOPS—CERAMIC TILE

MATERIAL CHARACTERISTICS

Ceramic tile is a fired or baked clay product with a hard and brittle glaze applied to the surface for color and/or texture. The manufacture of tile even in modern times remains more of an art than a science. Therefore, even if tile is manufactured to the strict tolerances the individual pieces will have some inherent flaws. Slight color variations from tile to tile will be typical in genuine glazed ceramic tiles. Also, due to the firing process there may be a slight surface variation, or it may not be perfectly flat. Ceramic tiles with a surface texture will, of course, vary in height.

Ceramic tile liners of specialty apron tiles are typically not manufactured by the same source as the field tile and therefore will vary from the field tile. Variation in size and or color within individual liners or within the shipment of liners may result in the appearance of unevenness in the finished product.

Variable job site conditions, variations and irregularities of the tile or stone will require decisions on layout, installation techniques and grout joint widths. The installers will make these decisions at the time of installation and at their sole discretion. In the event there is a different method of installation available, as determined by a third party, it will not render the original installation to be considered defective.

Grouting the joints between tiles will complete the installation of the ceramic tile countertop. There are two common types of grout joint installations. If the tiles are butted together to create a separation of not more than 1/8 inch in width, then an unsanded polyblend grout is used. If the joint between the tiles is set at 1/8 inch in width, then an unsanded polyblend grout is used. If the joint between the tiles is set at 1/8 inch to 1/2 inch in width, the grouting is done with a sanded polyblend grout. Colored grouts for either application may vary in shade from the sample used to select the color due to the wide variety of tiles available, environmental conditions and finishing techniques. The elements of nature, including but not limited to sun, temperature, food or chemical reactions, may combine with aging process to change the color of the grout in varying degrees over time.

Certain areas of colored grout on any given countertop area may also vary in color. If repair or replacement of tile or grout areas is required, matching the original or changed color of the remaining color tile grout may be impossible. Colored grout can also cause the discoloration, flecking and/or cracked appearance of the ceramic tile in the areas where colored grout is used. If grout is replaced, there is no guarantee that the replacement color will match that of the original installation.

Efflorescence (a whitish powder) can appear on the joints or along the edges of the tiles. This is a chemical reaction of soluble salts and water, common to all cement products. This material is harmless and can be removed by using a stiff bristle brush with clean water. It may take some time before it will completely disappear through normal use.

Separations and cracks in the grout between the tiles and between those tiles and backsplashes, bathtubs, shower pans, etc. are normal and are not covered by the warranty. Repair of cracked grout is considered a Homeowner maintenance item. The cracks can be repaired with a prepared and pre-mixed grout purchased from a paint or hardware store.

Settlement of the house and/or expansion or contraction of the tile substrate may also cause hairline cracks in ceramic tile or grout. This is considered normal and these tiles and/or grout cracks are not covered under warranty.

MAINTENANCE GUIDELINES

1. All ceramic tile surfaces installed in your new home are unsealed. The application of a sealer specifically formulated for use with this particular material, as recommended by the manufacturer, is highly advisable. There are several products available with varying Material Characteristics. Follow product instructions for application and maintenance. It is advisable to test an area which is not visible to make sure you are satisfied with the product and the results
2. Ceramic tile may be cleaned daily with a damp cloth or mop. Extremely dirty areas may be cleaned with a "natural" cleaner and water. Do not use any type of cleansers which contain chemicals or abrasives. Do not use steel wool, acids, or metallic brushes on the tile or grout as damage may result.
3. No waxing or polishing of ceramic tile is needed. You may use one-half teaspoon full of lemon oil sprinkled on soft cloth to remove hard water spots and restore shine to your new tile. Do not do this more frequently than one (1) time per month.
4. Always clean up liquid spills and water accumulations as soon as detected, to avoid staining and penetration of moisture through the grout. If the grout becomes stained, use a mild/diluted bleaching solution or a pre-mixed product, such as Soft Scrub with Bleach. Always rinse thoroughly and wipe with a soft cloth, being careful not to let the bleach solution drip or accumulate onto any adjacent surfaces, which could cause further damage. For colored grouts, color stains and paints are available from ceramic tile stores which can give your grout surface a like-new appearance.

5. To repair cracked grout between tiles, obtain the proper type and color of grout from a home improvement center. The grout may be available pre-mixed. In either case, follow the manufacturer's instructions for use. After the replacement of the grout, wash the area several times with warm water and a sponge to remove the haze residue left behind by the grout. Do not use harsh cleaning agents, steel wool pads, etc., which can scratch or damage the surface of your tile. Do not wash excess grout down the drain, which could cause blockage and cause the need for plumbing repairs.
6. For repair of cracked grout joints at tiled tubs or shower pans, it is typical to fill this joint with a silicone-based caulk available from your home improvement store. There may be repeated movement between the ceramic tile and tub or shower pan due to shrinkage in the framing materials, and a silicone based caulk will maintain flexibility and be less prone to further cracking. When caulk is applied in these locations, it will need to be redone from time to time.

COUTERTOPS—CULTURED MARBLE

MATERIAL CHARACTERISTICS

To avoid staining of cultured marble surfaces, do not allow spilled personal care products (cosmetics, perfumes, locations, etc.) to remain on the counter.

MAINTENANCE GUIDELINES

1. Clean the cultured marble surface periodically with mild soap and water. Never use abrasive cleaners and/or scouring pads.
2. Automobile wax can be applied as water repellent and to provide a shine, or as recommended by the manufacturer.

COUNTERTOPS—MANUFACTURED SOLID SURFACE

MATERIAL CHARACTERISTICS

You may have selected a manufactured solid surface material such as "DuPont Corian" for countertop installation in your home. Special care is required to keep your manufactured solid surface countertops in "as new" condition. Please refer to the Manufacturer's recommendations for care and maintenance guidelines.

The darker jewel tone and/or designer colors used on solid surface counters are higher maintenance than the lighter, translucent colors which are recommended for normal and high usage work surfaces. The darker colors will show dust, marks and scratches from normal use, more so than the lighter colors. The darker colors are meant to be used as accent materials rather than for use as the main work surface, and are therefore not recommended in instances where higher maintenance will be a concern.

MATERIAL GUIDELINES

1. See Manufacturer's guidelines for instructions on the maintenance of your specific product.

COUNTERTOPS—MARBLE AND STONE

MATERIAL CHARACTERISTICS

Marble/natural stone is a product of nature exhibiting unique color and texture variations in each piece, and no two pieces will be exactly the same. Variations of color, shading, veining, texture, pattern, thickness and marbling, as well as natural imperfections (such as pitting, scaling, fissures or factory filler) are all considered normal. No guarantees are made that the sample presented to the homebuyer for selection will match the actual material to be installed; the display sample will only exhibit the average color, texture, shading and marking of the natural stone.

If selecting a marble or stone tile (as opposed to a slab installation) for a countertop, please be aware the tiles cannot match slab material and vise versa. Stone moldings will also not match stone tiles or slab exactly and are subject to the same shading, texture, veining and other natural variances. Because of imperfect quarrying methods the overall dimension of the pieces may not be exact, which will cause variation in the grout lines. Variation in thickness of the pieces will cause height differences between the tiles which is considered normal.

Slab granite is a heavy natural stone material quarried from earth. No two slabs are alike. Each slab will have inherent variations; color, shading veining, pitting, fissures and textures. No two pieces of stone will ever look exactly the same even when cut from the same block of material. The natural products installed in your home will look different from the showroom samples and model installations.

Granite and natural stone products may crack from time to time for reasons that are not due to mishandling or poor installation. In any event, when a portion of slab requires replacement whether through fault of installation or not, the method of fixing the damage will be at the Builder's discretion. The Builder will endeavor to match the existing material as closely as possible, and a perfect match is never possible. The area of replacement may be limited to the area of the damage, either creating a new seam where the damaged material is replaced or replacing the material to the nearest seam. The Builder will attempt to match any materials that are replaced as closely as possible. Do not sit on countertops or place heavy tools upon them that may cause stress and cracks in the surface.

Marble/natural stones are considered very durable, and require maintenance. Periodic upkeep is recommended. Most stones are porous and readily absorb liquids and moisture, and will stain from any topical spill. All acids, including those found in many foods, fruits and beverages will likely etch the surface of polished stone, even if the stone has been sealed. Green marbled stone is especially susceptible to etching. In bath areas stone surfaces can also be susceptible to discoloration from soap, makeup products and hairsprays.

Variable job site conditions, variations and irregularities of the tile or stone require decisions on layout, installation techniques and grout joint widths. The installers will make these decisions at the time of installation.

Grouting the joints between tiles will complete the installation of the marble or stone tile countertop. There are two common types of grout joint installations. If the tiles are butted together to create a separation of not more than 1/8 inch in width, then an un-sanded polyblend grout is used. If the joint between the tiles is set at 1/8 inch to 1/2 inch in width, the grouting is done with a sanded polyblend grout.

Colored grouts for either application may vary in shade from the sample used to select the color due to the wide variety of tiles available, environmental conditions and finishing techniques. Light to mid-tone grout colors generally exhibits a tendency toward a wider shade variation than do dark colors. The elements of nature, including but not limited to sun, temperature, food or chemical reactions, may combine with aging process to change the color of the grout in varying degrees over time.

Certain areas of colored grout on any given countertop area may also vary in color. If repair or replacement of tile or grout areas is required, matching the original or changed color of the remaining colored grout may be impossible. Colored grout can also cause the discoloration, flecking and/or cracked appearance of the marble or stone tile in the areas where colored grout is used.

Use of colored grout with a stone surface may cause discoloration of the marble/natural stone due to the porosity of the material. The colored grout may also accentuate normal irregularities of the marble/stone.

Efflorescence (a whitish powder) can appear on the joints or along the edges of the tile. This is a chemical reaction of soluble salts and water, common to all cement products. This material is harmless and can be removed by using a stiff bristle brush with clean water. It may take some time before it will completely disappear through normal use.

Separations and cracks in the grout between the tiles and between those tiles and backsplashes, bathtubs, shower pants, etc. are normal. Repair of cracked grout is a Homeowner maintenance item. The cracks can be repaired with a pre-mixed grout purchased from a paint or hardware store.

Settlement of the house and/or expansion or contraction of the tile substrate may also cause hairline cracks in ceramic tile or grout. This is considered normal.

MAINTENANCE GUIDELINES

1. All marble/natural stone floor surfaces installed in your new home are unsealed. The application of a sealer specifically formulated for use with this particular material as recommended by the manufacturer is highly advisable. The sealer should be one which allows the stone to "breathe." There are several products available with varying material characteristics. Follow product instructions for application and maintenance. It is advisable to test an area which is not visible to make sure you are satisfied with the product and the results. Do not apply a grout sealer for a minimum of two (2) weeks after the date of installation.
2. Periodic cleaning of all stone surfaces with warm water is recommended to remove ordinary dirty and dust build up.
3. For more intensive cleaning, consult with the manufacturer of the stone for the type of cleaning product you should use specific to your stone.

4. Avoid the use of cleaning products which have distinctive colors, this includes oil based dressing or colored waxes. Over time, these tend to impart their character into the stone.
5. Avoid cleansers which contain grit or are highly alkaline in composition. Especially avoid mop and shine products typically obtained off of the grocer's shelf, as the alkaline will penetrate the surface of the material and then form crystals in the stone. The pressure exerted by the crystals will pop the stone leaking pits and gouges in the surface.
6. Always clean up liquid spill and water accumulations as soon as detected, to avoid staining and penetration of moisture through the grout into the substructure.
7. If the grouting becomes stained, use a mild bleaching solution (diluted to 1 part bleach to 4 parts water). Simply apply a small amount of this mixture and scrub with a soft bristly brush. Avoid contact of this mixture on the stone.
8. Colored grouts, color stains and paints are available from ceramic tiles stores which can give your grout surface a new appearance. Remember the colored stain may leach into the porous stone.
9. To repair cracked grout between tiles, obtain the proper type and color of grout from a home improvement center. The grout may be available pre-mixed. In either case, follow the manufacturer's instructions for use. After the replacement of the grout, wash the area several times with warm water and a sponge to remove the haze residue left behind by the grout. Do not use harsh cleaning agents, steel wood pads, etc., which can scratch or damage the surface of your tile. Be careful not to wash excess grout down the drain, which could cause blockage and cause the need for plumbing repairs.

10. For repair of cracked grout joints at tiled tubs or shower pans, it may be more effective to fill this joint with a silicone-based caulk available from your local home improvement store. There may be repeated movement between the ceramic tile and tub or shower pan due to shrinkage in the framing materials, and a silicone based caulk will maintain flexibility and be less prone to further cracking. A re-application of the caulk may be necessary from time to time.

ELECTRICAL

MATERIAL CHARACTERISTICS

A panel of circuit breakers protects the electrical wiring and circuits in your home. Circuit breakers are in the electrical panel located on the outside of the home, typically, near the front of the garage. The circuit breakers are labeled to indicate the room(s) or equipment which it controls. Depending on the size of the home, a sub panel may be located in the garage and will usually accommodate the lights/switches/plugs circuits only. The panel and circuit breakers should be identified for you during you New Home Orientation.

The capacity of the service panel has been specified to be more than adequate for daily use. However if you maintain a home office (using a computer, copier, printer, fax, etc.), or have other electrical equipment not found in the typical home, the service may not provide adequate amperage. Overloading (using too many appliances at one time), a defective cord, or starting an electric motor may cause electrical outlet failure. Electric motors require more current when starting, so it is a good idea to turn off a few lights before you turn the motor on.

Each circuit is destined to carry a limited amount of electrical current. If a circuit is overloaded by too many or too powerful an appliance or there is some other malfunction, the circuit breaker will be tripped to the "OFF" position. Before attempting to turn the circuit breaker back on, you should be certain there are no defects in cords or appliances, which draw their current form that circuit. To restore current, simply move the switch to the "ON" position. If power is not restored flip the breaker "OFF" and "ON" once or twice to insure the breaker is rest.

Ground fault Circuit interrupter ("GFCI") outlets are sensitive safety devices installed in the electrical system. The GFCI will "trip" or turn off the circuit if a danger of electrical shock or circuit overload exists. GFCI receptacles are located in water sensitive areas including the kitchen, bathrooms, outdoors, garage, etc. GFCI outlets are designed to "trip" for you protection - this will likely occur from time to time. If the outlet will not reset after a few attempts, do not continue to use the outlet until the "trip" cause is determined.

Do not plug your refrigerator or freezer into a GFCI outlet as it may "trip" due to the surge of the motor. A "tripped" garage outlet could go undetected for quite some time, which could result in food spoilage. If you have an irrigation timer plugged into the GFCI outlet, check the backup battery periodically to ensure power to the clock without disruption.

If there is a complete loss of power to the home, contact your local utility provider directly.

MAINTENANCE GUIDELINES

1. Check the GFCI outlets monthly for proper function. With a small appliance plugged into the GFCI outlet and running press the "test" button. The appliance should shut off. Press the "reset" button and the appliance should start running again. If this does not occur discontinue use of the outlet until the cause of the malfunction can be determined.
2. All lighting fixtures have bulb specifications imprinted on them. For safety and fixture longevity, use only the size and type bulb called for.
3. If you have small children, it is suggested outlets be covered with childproof plastic electrical wall outlet covers.

FLOORING-GENERAL

MATERIAL CHARACTERISTICS

Flooring surfaces were likely selected by the Homeowner during the process of purchasing your new home, including carpet and pad, ceramic tile, marble, stone, vinyl and wood.

At the time of purchase, your designer should have provided you with disclosures and specific information on the various flooring products that you have selected. You should take the time to read this important information because it provides guidelines necessary to maintain your manufacturer's warranties as well as care and maintenance suggestions. This information will also provide other specific product information about the warranties on your flooring selections. Please refer to the manufacturer's websites for further information.

It is a good idea to keep your flooring purchase documentation with your other warranty items just in case you need to request warranty service under the manufacturer's warranty. The manufacturer will request this information as proof of purchase and to validate your product warranties.

The uniqueness of material can make replacement and color matching difficult. If warranty service or repair work is required, portions of the original installation may have to be replaced. Your Builder will not be responsible for dye lot variations, discontinued patterns, discontinued ceramic or stone tile sizes, discontinued wood floor materials, lot shade variations, natural or manufactured material variations or grout color variations.

A variety of transition material types are used to separate different types of products. Variance in thickness of any given product will determine the type of transition to be used and reducers, such as vinyl or wood, are often used to help reduce any height difference. The Builder reserves the right to utilize a form of transition and a layout of the transition which best suits the types of flooring materials being installed.

When moving furniture and heavy appliances, lay a plywood panel on the floor and move the item across the panel. This protects your floors from scuffing, tearing and staining. As a general rule, the heavier the item, the more protection you will need.

With vinyl flooring, door not use rubber or latex-backed floor mats or rugs. These products have a potential to cause discoloration to your flooring. Select mats or rugs that are non-staining, are vinyl-backed or woven, and are colorfast. Even certain woven floor rugs may stain your new floor if they become moist or wet. These types of conditions are beyond the control of the Builder and require that the new homeowner pay close attention to prevent these potentially undesirable conditions.

MATERIAL GUIDELINES

1. See Manufacturer's guidelines for instructions on the maintenance of your specific product.

FLOORING-CARPET

MATERIAL CHARACTERISTICS

Carpet is a woven product of multiple layers of nylon and latex and in some cases wool or polypropylene. Refer to the Manufacturer's warranties for stain resistance qualities and warranties; however keep in mind, depending on the type of use and amount of foot traffic, all carpet will stain to some degree regardless of Manufactures' claims or warranties.

Carpet seaming will be selected by the carpet installer to be placed in the most unobtrusive location, depending on the width of the product selected and the dimension of the room where the carpet is installed. This is at the discretion of the installer. Depending on the type of carpet the seam will be more or less noticeable. The visibility of seams is a normal characteristic of carpet, and cannot be completely eliminated. As the carpet ages after the original installation, the seams will tend to relax and will become less noticeable over time.

Also as the carpet ages, it will be susceptible to fading from sunlight. Due to this condition, and the fact the shade color of the carpet will slightly vary from dye lot to dye lot, if a portion of the carpet has to be replaced due to repairs or misuse, the new replacement carpet will not be an exact match to the original carpet.

When the carpet is new, you may notice there will be quite a bit of shedding of loose carpet fibers. This is a normal condition. More frequent vacuuming may be needed at first to relieve this condition. Over time the shedding should abate and a normal vacuuming schedule can them be adhered to.

A special note regarding Berber and pattern carpets, Berber and pattern carpets are installed over a very firm pad of commercial type quality due to the stitching and seams. A perfect match at the seams may not be obtainable and seams are more noticeable with Berber and pattern carpet, especially the cross seams. The natural line of the Berber may not follow the line of the adjacent wall(s). Also, variations in weave may create a slightly wavy appearance, and seams may be more noticeable as a result.

MAINTENANCE GUIDELINES

1. To obtain the best performance and longest wear, adhere strictly to the care and maintenance recommended by the manufacturer, who has provided you with a care program to help preserve your carpet's appearance during its natural life expectancy.

2. A good vacuum cleaner is vital to prolonging the beauty and life of your carpet. An inexpensive machine can remove the surface dirt but will not effectively remove the hidden dirt and particles embedded in the pile. Most Manufacturers recommend the use of vacuums with a rotating brush or a combination of a beater/brush/bar which agitates the carpet tile and mechanically loosens soil for removal by the vacuum.
3. Initially test your vacuum cleaner in an inconspicuous place, such as in a closet, to find the settings which work the best and are correct for your type of carpet. Settings which are too aggressive for the type of carpet can cause fuzzing or deterioration of the nap. By using the proper setting when you vacuum you can reduce the wear of the carpet.
4. Note: carpet with a thick loop pile construction may be sensitive to brushing or rubbing of the pile surface and may become fuzzy. For these types of carpet products, it is recommended the Homeowner use a vacuum with suction-only or a unit with an adjustable brush lifted away from the carpet so it does not agitate the pile.
5. Remove spots and stains according to Manufacturer's guidelines and as soon as they are discovered.
6. Use doormats at your home's entryways to absorb soil and moisture. Keep in mind all mats will stain if moisture is trapped, and as a result they may cause staining to the underlying surface. An open weave natural fiber type of mat is best.
7. Alter traffic patterns and avoid excessive pile crushing by occasionally moving and rearranging heavy furniture.
8. Protect your carpet from prolonged periods of direct sunlight with window blinds or shades.
9. If you use area rugs over your carpet, remove and clean them regularly, restoring the carpet pile underneath. After cleaning your carpet, always allow for complete drying before replacing the area rugs. Note: area rugs can stain or discolor underlying carpet.

10. Professionally clean your carpet as soon as you notice color dulling. Be sure your carpet cleaning contractor is familiar with the Manufacturers' cleaning guidelines for your specific carpet.

FLOORING-CERAMIC TILE

MATERIAL CHARACTERISTICS

Ceramic tile is a fired of baked clay product with a hard and brittle glaze applied to the surface for color and/or texture. The manufacturer of tile even in modern times remains more of an art than a science. Therefore, even if tile is manufactured to strict tolerances, the individual pieces will still have some inherent flaws. Slight color variations from tile to tile will be typical in genuine glazed ceramic tiles. Also, due to the firing process there may be a slight surface variation, or it may not be perfectly flat. Ceramic tiles with a surface texture will, of course, vary in height.

Grouting the joints between tiles will complete the installation of the ceramic tile countertop. Color grouts for either application may vary in shade from the sample used to select the color due to the wide variety of tiles available, environmental conditions and finishing techniques. The elements of nature, including but not limited to sun, temperature, food or chemical reactions, may combine with aging process to change the color of the grout in varying degrees over time.

Certain areas of colored grout on any given floor area may also vary in color. If repair or replacement of tile or grout areas is required, matching the original or changed color of the remaining colored grout may be impossible. Colored grout can also cause discoloration, flecking and/or cracked appearance of the ceramic tile in the areas where colored grout is used.

Separations and cracks in the grout between the tiles and between those tiles and baseboards, thresholds, backsplashes, bathtubs, shower pans, etc. are considered normal. Repair of cracked grout is a Homeowner maintenance item. The cracks can be repaired with a pre-mixed grout purchased from a paint or hardware store.

Settlement of the house and/or expansion or contraction of the tile substrate may also cause hairline cracks in ceramic tile or grout. This is considered normal.

MAINTENANCE GUIDELINES

1. All ceramic tile surfaces installed in your new home are unsealed. The application of a sealer specifically formulated for use with this particular material as recommended by the manufacturer is highly advisable. There are several products available with varying Material Characteristics. Follow product instructions for application and maintenance. It is advisable to test an area which is not visible to make sure you are satisfied with the product and the results.
2. Ceramic tile may be cleaned daily with a damp cloth or mop. Extremely dirty areas may be cleaned with a "natural" cleaner and water. Do not use any type of cleansers which contain chemicals or abrasives. Do not use steel wool, acids, or metallic brushes on the tile or grout, as damage may result.
3. No waxing or polishing of ceramic tile is needed. You may use one-half teaspoon full of lemon oil or red oil sprinkled on a soft cloth to remove hard water spots and restore shine to your new tile. Do not do this more frequently than once per month.
4. Always clean up liquid spills and water accumulation as soon as detected, to avoid staining and penetration of moisture through the grout into the substructure.
5. Use doormats at your home's entryways to absorb soil and moisture. Keep in mind all mats will stain if moisture is trapped and as a result they may cause staining to the underlying surface. An open weave natural fiber type of mat is best.

6. If the grout becomes stained, use a mild/diluted bleaching solution or a pre-mixed product, such as Soft Scrub with Bleach. Always rinse thoroughly and wipe with a soft cloth, being careful not to let the bleach solution drip or accumulate onto any adjacent surfaces, which could cause further damage.
7. For colored grouts, color stains are available from ceramic tile stores which can give your grout surface a new appearance.
8. To repair cracked grout between tiles and tiles at baseboard, obtain the proper type and color of grout from a home improvement center. The grout may be available pre-mixed. In either case, follow the manufacturers' instructions for use.
9. Following any grout replacement, wash the area several times with warm water and a sponge to remove the haze residue left behind by the grout.
10. Do not use harsh cleaning agents, steel wool pads, etc., which can scratch or damage the surface of your tile. Be careful not to wash excess grout down the drain, which could cause blockage and cause the need for plumbing repairs.
11. For repair of cracked grout joints at tiled tubs or shower pans, it may be more effective to fill this joint with a silicone-based caulk available from your home improvement store. There may be repeated movement between the ceramic tile and tub or shower pan due to shrinkage in the framing materials, and a silicone based caulk will maintain flexibility and be less prone to further cracking.

FLOORING-MARBLE AND STONE

MATERIAL CHARACTERISTICS

Marble and natural stone are products of nature, exhibiting unique color and texture variations in each piece, and no two pieces will be exactly the same. Variations of color, shading, veining, thickness and marbling, as well as natural imperfections are all considered normal. Also, because of imperfect quarrying methods the overall dimension of the pieces may not be exact, which will cause variation in the grout lines. Variation in thickness of the pieces will cause height differences between the tiles and is also considered normal.

Marble/natural stones are considered very durable, and although they require little maintenance, periodic upkeep is recommended. Most stones are porous and readily absorb liquids and moisture, and will stain from any topical spill. All acids, including those found in many foods, fruits and beverages will likely etch the surface of polished stone, even if the stone has been sealed. Green marbles are especially susceptible to etching. In bath areas stone surfaces can also be susceptible to discoloration from soap, makeup products and hairsprays.

Grouting the joints between tiles will complete the installation of the ceramic tile floor. Natural gray grout will be relatively uniform in color and is the easiest grout to maintain and repair.

Colored grouts may vary in shade form the sample used to select the color due to the wide variety of tiles available, environmental conditions and finishing techniques. The elements of nature, including but not limited to sun, temperature, food or chemical reactions, may combine with aging process to change the color of the grout in varying degrees over time.

Use of colored grout with a stone surface may cause discoloration of the marble/natural stone due to the porosity of the material. The colored grout may also accentuate normal irregularities of the marble/stone.

Certain areas of colored grout on any given floor area may also vary in color. IF repair or replacement of tile or gout areas is required, matching the original or changed color of the remaining colored grout may be impossible. Colored grout can also cause the discoloration; flecking and/or cracked appearance of the ceramic tile in the areas where colored grout is used.

Separations and cracks in the grout between the tiles and between those tiles and baseboards, thresholds, backsplashes, bathtubs, shower pans, etc. are normal. Repair of cracked grout is a Homeowner maintenance item. The cracks can be repaired with a pre-mixed grout purchased from a paint or hardware store.

Settlement of the house and/or expansion or contraction of the tile substrate may also cause hairline cracks in ceramic tile or grout. This is considered normal.

MAINTENANCE GUIDELINES

1. All marble/natural stone floor surfaces installed in your new home are unsealed. The application of a sealer specifically formulated for use with this particular material as recommended by the manufacturer is highly advisable.
2. If you apply a sealer, it should be one which allows the stone to "breathe." There are several products available. Follow product instructions for applications and maintenance. It is advisable to test an area which is not visible to make sure you are satisfied with the product and the results.
3. Dry mop floors frequently to sweep up dirty and grit. Grit causes scratches on polished marble. Also, particles of asphalt or tar tacked on floors contain oil. Highly alkaline cleaning products are apt to dissolve or emulsify the oily matter and carry it into the marble, causing stains, which are hard to remove.
4. Periodic cleaning of all stone surfaces with warm water is recommended to remove ordinary dirt and dust build up.
5. For more intensive cleaning, consult with the manufacturer of the stone for the type of cleaning product you should use specific to your stone.
6. Avoid the use of cleaning products which have distinctive colors, this includes oil based dressing or colored waxes. Over time, these tend to impart their character into the stone.

7. Avoid cleansers which contain grit or are highly alkaline in composition. Mop and shine products typically obtained off of the grocer's shelf especially are to be avoided as the alkaline will penetrate the surface of the material and then form crystals in the stone. The pressure exerted by the crystals will pop the stone leaving pits and gouges in the surface.
8. Use doormats at your home's entryways to absorb soil and moisture. Keep in mind all mats will stain if moisture is trapped and as a result they may cause staining to the underlying surface. It is best to place the mats outside the entry doors. An open weave natural fiber type of mat is best, however be careful to select woven mats labeled "colorfast" to prevent the potential of staining from colored dyes used by the manufacturer.
9. Always clean up liquid spills and water accumulations as soon as detected, to avoid staining and penetration of moisture through the grout into the substructure.
10. If the grouting becomes stained, use a mild bleaching solution (diluted to 1 part bleach to 4 parts water). Simply apply a small amount of this mixture and scrub with a soft bristle brush. **Avoid contact of this mixture on the stone.**
11. For colored grouts, color stains are available from ceramic tile stores which can give your grout surface a new appearance. Remember the colored stain may leach into the porous stone.
12. To repair cracked grout between tiles and tiles at baseboard, obtain the proper type and color of grout from a home improvement center. The grout may be available pre-mixed. In either case, follow the manufacturer's instructions for use. After the replacement of the grout, wash the area several times with warm water and a sponge to remove the haze residue left behind the grout.
13. Do not use harsh cleaning agents, steel wool pads, etc., which can scratch or damage the surface of your tile. Be careful not to wash excess grout down the drain, which could cause blockage and cause the need for plumbing repairs.

14. For repair of cracked grout joints at tiled tubs or shower pans, it may be more effective to fill this joint with a silicone-based caulk available from your home improvement store. There may be repeated movement between the ceramic tile and tub or shower pan due to shrinkage in the framing materials, and a silicone based caulk will maintain flexibility and be less prone to further cracking.
15. Do not move heavy objects across marble/natural stone floors as breakage may result. Also, do not use handcarts or any other equipment with wheels on the surface as this may cause scratching, scoring or breakage.

FLOORING-VINYL

MATERIAL CHARACTERISTICS

Vinyl is the softest material of the hard surface floor products and is highly susceptible to dents, scratches, staining and scuffing. Nevertheless, it is effective flooring and is often used in areas where water and spills are likely, such as the kitchen, laundry and bath areas.

This type of flooring material will provide years of service when properly maintained. Pay close attention to the Manufacturer's Warranty and Care and Maintenance Guidelines. Vinyl flooring can be susceptible to heavy usage so proper care is crucially important.

MAINTENANCE GUIDELINES

1. Sweep or vacuum frequently to prevent dirt particles from being ground into the surface of the vinyl flooring.
2. Wipe up spills immediately to avoid staining.
3. To clean, use a damp mop and clean water to lightly wash the flooring surfaces weekly. If desired use one teaspoon of vinegar or Windex mixed with each gallon of water.

4. IF the flooring surfaces receive hard use and become extremely dirty, use a mild detergent in the mop water, and apply the detergent solution to the floor with a sponge mop. After the soil deposits have been loosened, mop up excess detergent and water. Rinse the mop thoroughly with clear water to remove all of the detergent, and then rinse the floor using the clean mop with fresh, warm water to remove the soapy residue. Any detergent film left on the floor can hold tracked-in dirt and leave the surface with a dull, cloudy appearance.
5. Avoid solvent-based cleaners, abrasive cleaners, or wax.
6. Do not use rubber-backed or latex-backed floor rugs or mats on your vinyl floors. These products may potentially stain or discolor your vinyl flooring. Refer to the tags on your rugs for labeling such as "colorfast" and "non-staining"; these qualities will prevent potential problems with discoloration.
7. Use doormats at your home's entryways to absorb soil and moisture. Keep in mind all mats will stain if moisture is trapped and as a result they may cause staining to the underlying surface. An open weave natural fiber type of mat is best.
8. Avoid the wearing of pointed or black heels on vinyl flooring. The concentrated weight will leave dents in the surface and black heels may stain or mark the surface.
9. Exposure to direct sunlight on your floor for prolonged periods can cause fading. During peak sunlight hours, the use of drapes or blinds is recommended.
10. Protect your floor against burns from cigarettes, matches and extremely hot items.
11. Resilient-flooring material will tear if heavy appliances, such as refrigerators, washers or dryers, are improperly moved across the surface. Use appropriate appliance dollies. Heavy furniture should be placed on pads to avoid point loads, such as sofa legs or piano legs, from penetrating the surface.

12. If installed in a bathroom, inspect the joint between the vinyl flooring and the toilet as well as the joint between the flooring and the tub or shower on a monthly basis. Touchup any gaps or shrinkage in the caulking as needed.

FLOORING – WOOD

MATERIAL CHARACTERISTICS

Wood floor material is a product of nature and will contain natural imperfections. The material has been manufactured in accordance with accepted industry standards. Imperfections may be a result of manufacturing (within acceptable tolerances) or it may be a natural characteristic of the wood. The Industry accepted stains, waxes, fillers or putty sticks will be used for cosmetically correcting imperfections during installation of the floor.

Height variation may occur between floorboards due to a difference in material heights and sub-floor undulation. Separation between boards may also vary due to temperature and humidity related expansion and contraction.

Mod wood floor material used today is laminate flooring. Laminate flooring is a high-pressured engineered composite, consisting of layers of wood fused together to provide a wear and impact resistant surface. The core layer resists swelling and indentation and provides stability. The backing provides structural balance and added strength. The tongue and groove bonding is a floating floor installation system. This floating floor installation may flex and create a hollow sound when walked on. The floor will be installed per the Manufacturer's requirements, and the proper installation may include the separation of large areas with a T-molding to allow for proper expansion and contraction.

All laminate flooring is susceptible to dents, cracks and scratches. Scratches cannot be rejuvenated like a solid wood floor. To protect the floor from scratching, follow the maintenance guidelines from the flooring manufacturer.

Please note pre-finished wood floors will not match the stain on other items such as cabinets.

MAINTENANCE GUIDELINES

1. Vacuum or dust mop at the same frequency as for carpeting.
2. A damp (not a wet) mop can be used for spills on floors which have a non-waxed polyurethane finish (always follow the damp mop with a dry cloth to insure no moisture is left on the wood surface).
3. Some scuffing should be expected in areas of heavy traffic. If the floor is waxed, occasional buffing helps remove scuffmarks. A waxed floor should only be re-waxed per the recommendations provided by the manufacturer.
4. No matter what type of finish is on your wood floor, never intentionally pour water directly on the floor. While damp mopping is fine for non-waxed polyurethane finishes in good condition, excessive amounts of water may find a way of seeping between the boards, causing stains or warping (always follow the damp mop with a dry cloth to insure no moisture is left on the wood surface).
5. Use doormats at your home's entryways to absorb soil and moisture. Keep in mind that all mats will stain if moisture is trapped and as a result they may cause staining to the underlying surface. An open weave natural fiber type of mat is best.
6. Avoid the wearing of high heels on wood flooring. The concentrated weight will leave dents in the surface.
7. Exposure to direct sunlight on your floor for prolonged periods can cause fading. During peak sunlight hours, the use of drapes or blinds is recommended.
8. Throw rugs or area rugs left in one location for an extended period of time may cause discoloration or uneven fading to the wood finish.
9. Protect your floor against burns from cigarettes, matches and extremely hot items.

10. Wood flooring material will dent and/or splinter if heavy appliances, such as refrigerators, washers or dryers, are improperly moved across the surface. Use appropriate appliance dollies.
11. At a minimum all furniture placed on wood floors should use felt protectors on furniture legs. Heavy furniture should be placed on pads to avoid point loads, such as sofa legs or piano legs, from indenting the surface.

FOOD DISPOSAL

MATERIAL CHARACTERISTICS

Your disposal is self-cleaning and self-contained, needing no maintenance or lubrication of the motor. Because it is a consumer product, you must complete and mail in the warranty registration card for service. For optimum performance with the least amount of wear and tear, run plenty of cold water when using the disposal.

If the disposal will not start, follow the instructions as provided by the manufacturer in combination with the following information.

MAINTENANCE GUIDELINES

1. Always use cold water when the disposal is operating
2. Use the disposal sparingly to maximize the disposal life.
3. Do not grind extremely fibrous food materials such as certain meats, vegetables and fruit rinds, artichokes, celery or cornhusks as they will plug the drain and may cause a blockage or jam of the disposal.
4. To clean the disposal, fill the sink with cold water, turn on the disposal and remove the stopper. While the water is draining through the disposal, allow the tap to continue running. When the sink is empty, the disposal will be clean.
5. Odors can be caused over time by accumulation of food particles or grease in the grind chamber. This buildup may be a result of insufficient water flow during and after use of the disposal.

6. The disposal unit can be "freshened up" with a small ice cubes which are a solution of one (1) cup of vinegar per tray of water. Start the disposal and add a tray of vinegar ice cubes. After the grinding action is completed, flush the disposal with cold water. Grinding lemon peels will also help with masking odors.
7. Never put lye or other chemical drainpipe cleaners into the disposal unit, as they will cause serious corrosion of any alloy parts. This will also void all guarantees and warranties.

OPERATING GUIDELINES

1. Do not overload the disposal
2. Always operate the disposal with the splashguard in place and according to the manufacturer's operating and troubleshooting instructions.
3. Before calling for service you should check the following:
    a. Loud noises- when the unit and water is completely off, remove the splash guard, as needed, and use tongs to investigate for and remove any foreign objects. Replace the splashguard. Never insert your hand into the disposal.
    b. Unit does not start or is jammed- Use the hex wrench provided with the unit to reverse the disposal teeth. The hex nut is located under the disposal unit. When the disposal turns freely, push the red reset button and then turn the disposal on.
        i. If the previous effort is unsuccessful, check with a screwdriver or broom handle to see if the turntable inside the unit rotates freely

ii. If the turntables move freely, check the reset button. If it has been tripped, push it back in until you hear a click, and it remains depressed. If the rest button is not tripped, check the following in this order: a) shorted or broken wire connected to the unit; b) wall switch for loose connection; c) fuse box/circuit breaker. Further action will require a qualified repair person to keep the warranty intact.
iii. If the turntable is stuck, check for a foreign object lodged between the turntable and the grind ring. Dislodge by rotating turntable with a pry bar, screw driver, de-jamming tool or broom handle. Remove the foreign object. Further action will require a qualified repair person to keep the warranty intact.

PAINTED SURFACES – INTERIOR

MATERIAL CHARACTERISTICS

The walls, woodwork and other interior painted components of your home have been painted with the appropriate type of paint product depending upon their use. It is typical for the woodwork, kitchen walls, bathroom walls and utility room walls have been painted with semi-gloss paint. All other walls have been painted with interior flat paint.

Your home may include stain grade woods in some locations such as for stairs, entry doors, etc. Unlike furniture building, in the construction of homes the stain grade wood components are not matched for similarities. It is expected there will be variations in hardness, grain and color of the natural wood and the species of woods may not even be specified to match between the entry door, stair railing, cabinets, etc. These variations will dictate how the stain will reappear on the finished surface. The finish may not necessarily be even in appearance. Also, color matching between wood parts and components cannot be guaranteed even when using the same stain color. These variations are natural material characteristics of real wood.

The chemical composition of all paint and stain is affected by climatic conditions. Over time, the finish might fade, dull and/or yellow. This is a natural aging process. You may find the kitchen and baths require more frequent re-painting than the rest of your home due to steam condensation and more frequent usage. For a consistent color match when repainting or refinishing, have your paint supplier or home improvement center color match with a chip taken from the surface you are planning to touch up or repaint.

When you redecorate or repaint the interior of the home, you should re-review and keep in mind the material characteristics of drywall. As previously noted, drywall will have some inherent flaws and blemishes which are considered normal; seams or joints which are noticeable, slight wave or unevenness in the wallboard, uneven texture, etc. When a flat paint is applied to the walls it tends to de-emphasize the inconsistencies in the drywall finish as flat paint absorbs light instead of reflecting it. If these surfaces are painted with a semi-gloss or gloss paint, the inconsistencies in the drywall will be accentuated due to the light reflection. If a semi-gloss or gloss finish is desired, you should consult with a professional painter to properly prepare the surface and minimize the inconsistencies.

MAINTENANCE GUIDELINES

1. A move-in paint kit is typically supplied with your new home and contains enough paint to make minor touch ups to the interior paint. It is a good idea to keep these cans after the paint is gone and to make a note listing the paint manufacturer and paint codes so you can purchase additional paint at a later date.
2. On painted or laminated surfaces use only a mild soap with warm water for necessary cleaning. Do not use brushes or abrasives, which can scratch or remove paint.

3. Minor cracks at room corners or around windows and doors are normal and are part of Homeowner maintenance out outlined in the DRYWALL section of this guide. Following the technique suggested for repair of minor cracks, it is possible paint touchup can be avoided.
4. Flat wall paint may not be necessarily washable. Before washing a large area which is needed, it is a good idea to experiment with washing on an area which is not highly visible such as in a closet.

PLUMBING - FAUCETS

MATERIAL CHARACTERISTICS

Refer to the PRODUCT LITERATURE & MANUFACTUER'S WARRANTIES section for terms of the Warranty on your faucets. Contact your Builder's Customer Service Department if you have questions about the type(s) of faucets installed in your home.

The best way to prolong faucet life is to avoid force when turning off the water. Unnecessary force may cut or otherwise damage "O" rings, washers, sleeves or seats and require premature replacement of the entire faucet. Normal hand pressure should result in a full shutoffs of water flow and drips. Loose or worn washers usually cause noisy pipes and faucets, as well as drips.

If your sink faucet has a removal spray nozzle, take car to never let water flow back into the opening where the nozzle is seated. This situation could possibly occur when filling large pots, pans, fish bowls, etc. and if the sink if used for bathing of children, pets or otherwise. Water entering through the opening may potentially damage contents in the cabinet below of the cabinet itself. You should take care to prevent this situation as damage to the cabinet or contents will not be repaired or replaced by your builder under the warranty.

If a sink faucet develops a leak, turn the water valve stop to the OFF position. The water valve stop is located underneath the sink.

For a tub or shower faucet leak within the wall, turn off the house water supply at the main valve control and notify your Builder's Customer Service Department or a professional plumber, as appropriate. Shutoff valve locations should have been demonstrated to you at your New Home Orientation. Please call your Builder's Customer Service Department if you have any questions regarding these locations.

MAINTENANCE GUIDELINES

1. Use only a soft cloth to clean and shine all handles and decorative finishes. Using polish, detergents, abrasive cleaners, organic solvents or acid may cause damage.
2. Replace valve gaskets, as necessary, disassembling the faucet according to the Manufacturer's guidelines. Use only specified replacement parts for repairs. **Note:** Always turn-off the water supply and relieve pressure before working on your faucet.
3. A leaking faucet may result from a worn out washer or from excessive sediment collected on the valve seat. Replacement stem assembly cartridges can be purchased at any plumbing supply store.
4. Remove (unscrew) the aerator (the screen device located where the water exists the faucet) and flush out any foreign objects to maintain a smooth water flow every six (6) months, or as necessary.
5. If the water heater, garden or washing machine faucet valves leak at the base of the handle, tighten the packing nut located on the top of the valve and add more packing if needed.

PLUMBING-PORCELAIN FIXTURES

MATERIAL CHARACTERISTICS

Porcelain plumbing fixtures (bathtubs, toilets and sinks) are designed to stay looking new for years with only a minimum amount of care. To preserve the beauty and gloss of porcelain bathtubs, toilets and sinks, observe one basic rule: NEVER USE ABRASIVE CLEANERS. Abrasive cleaners scratch through glasslike surfaces quickly. Liquid dishwashing detergent on a moist cloth is the preferred method of cleaning.

Although porcelain is durable, take care not to drop heavy articles on it, which might cause chipping. Should chipping occur, porcelain repair services are available. Contact you Builder's Customer Service Department if you have questions about this.

Since water is being used in these fixtures, it is important the joints between the fixtures and the surrounding waterproof surfaces remain sealed. If the seal is not maintained and water is allowed to seep into the joint, there is a possibility of damage to the underlying structure or other component of the home, and it also creates an environment for mold to grow.

MAINTENANCE GUIDELINES

1. Avoid abrasive cleaners and solvents which may ruin porcelain and plastic parts. Clean with a soft, damp cloth and dishwashing detergent, followed by brisk polishing with a clean, dry cloth.
2. Check the joint between the porcelain fixture and the supporting surface periodically for gaps or separation. Use a silicone-based caulk to seal the gaps as needed.

PLUMBING – TUB & SHOWER

MATERIAL CHARACTERISTICS

The tub installed in your home is going to be either a fiberglass tub or a steel tub with a porcelain finish. Both types of tubs will provide years of service if properly maintained.

Fiberglass tubs have a gel coat surface which can crack or scratch if used improperly. However, if damage occurs there are professional re-finishers to be found online, or in your local

Yellow Pages which can repair or re-finish the tub to appear as new. Over a long period of time the gel coat may become thin and wear through to the fiberglass, however this is easily remedied by having the tub refinished in place. Also, water in certain regional areas, if not wiped up after bathing/showering, may cause fading or staining of the tub/shower color coat.

Steel tubs have a porcelain finish which is susceptible to scratches or chips if used improperly. There are professional refinishers which can repair or refinish the tub in the event some damage should occur. If combined with a shower installation, the shower surround will typically be installed using ceramic tile.

For the stand-alone shower (without a tub), it may have been installed using a fiberglass stall, or by combining a fiberglass pan or tile pan with a tile surround. The fiberglass shower will have the same material characteristics as the tub.

Maintain your bath and shower areas regularly to prevent mold and mildew build-up and water leakage into the wall spaces. Water which escapes the tub/shower after bathing should be wiped up immediately. The tub/shower area should also be well ventilated during and between uses to allow moisture to dry completely.

MAINTENANCE GUIDELINES

1. Keep the room ventilated by opening doors and windows for cross ventilation when the room is not in use and after use of the tub and/or shower.
2. If your tub/shower is fiberglass, use only a mild, non-abrasive liquid detergent solution to clean it. If water scale has been allowed to build up, attempt to clean it only using a natural product, do not use chemicals which may dull and/or etch the finish surface. There are special bathroom cleaners available which are specifically formulated for use on fiberglass tubs and showers.

3. You can protect and restore the gloss by applying an acrylic polish or automotive paste wax. Minor scratches can be buffed out using an automotive polishing compound and then following up with a coat of wax. Deep scratches, should they occur, will require professional restoration.
4. Inspect the joint(s) where the fiberglass tub/shower joins the drywall periodically and touch up any shrinkage or gaps in the caulking as needed. Remove and replace any caulking which is showing signs of mildew.
5. Inspect the shower head arm where it penetrates the wall by sliding the escutcheon down and looking for gaps or shrinkage in the caulking. Also check the escutcheons around the valve control(s) to ensure there are no gaps in the caulking. Re-caulk or grout as necessary.
6. To help keep your tile shower and bathtub enclosure walls mildew-free, clean them regularly with a tile cleaner. And frequently use a mold/mildew remover such as chlorine bleach and water solution (1 part bleach to 4 parts water). Be careful not to mix products which are not compatible such as ammonia and bleach.
7. Inspect the joint at the tub to tile location periodically. Touchup shrinkage and gaps by cleaning and filling the dry joint with a flexible caulking compound such as silicone rubber, according to the manufacturer's directions.
8. If you use a rubber or plastic "anti-skid" mat, make sure to remove it from the tub or shower after use to avoid harm to the surface finish.

SHOWER ENCLOSURE

MATERIAL CHARACTERISTICS

There are two (2) different styles of shower doors, either of which may be installed in your home. Bypass sliders operate similar to wardrobe doors. Other shower doors are hinged and operate much like any other standard door found in your home.

The door systems are designed with flanges and/or gaskets which are designed to keep most but not all of the water from the shower from escaping the enclosure. On bypass door enclosures make certain the doors are aligned properly. When standing in the shower the overlapping door (from the inside) should be closest to the showerhead.

It is important to note the shower enclosure does not waterproof the shower from the rest of the room. It is likely some water is going to escape. You can help alleviate some of this problem by pointing the showerhead away from the enclosure as much as possible. After each shower it is important to wipe up any water which may have escaped from the enclosure, as well as monitoring to make certain all adjacent surfaces are drying completely between showers in order to avoid mold or mildew. Clean glass enclosures frequently in order to avoid buildup of water spots.

MAINTENANCE GUIDELINES

1. Allow for proper ventilation.
2. You will be able to maintain the shower enclosure appearance for years with periodic cleaning. Use a mild soap and water to clean the metal frames. Do not use abrasive cleaners or scouring pads.
3. Clean window glass with a sponge and water or a commercial window cleaner.
4. Check the silicone seal around the sides and sill of the enclosure to insure the seal is intact. Touchup with a clear silicone sealant as needed. Avoid sealing drain holes in the shower enclosure as they are intended to allow water to run-off and escape the track.

SHOWER WALLS – CERAMIC TILE

MATERIAL CHARACTERISTICS

See the section titled **COUNTERTOPS – CERAMIC TILE** for the material characteristics of your ceramic tile shower walls.

MAINTENANCE GUIDELINES

1. Allow for proper ventilation.
2. For the other maintenance guidelines see the section titled COUTERTOPS – CERAMIC TILE.
3. Inspect the top of the ceramic tile shower surround for gaps or shrinkage in the caulking between the tile and drywall surface. Re-caulk or grout as necessary. Also look to see water is not allowed to pool in a pocket or depression in the caulk or grout, which can be a location for mold growth. Fill the depression with caulk or grout until the surface is sloped toward the face of the tile surround.
4. Inspect the shower head arm where it penetrates the wall by sliding the escutcheon down and looking for gaps or shrinkage in the caulking. Also check the escutcheons around the valve control(s) to ensure there are no gaps in the caulking. Re-caulk or grout as necessary.

SMOKE DETECTORS

MATERIAL CHARACTERISTICS

A 110- volt smoke detector system with a battery backup is on every floor, in each bedroom, and in each hall which adjoins a bedroom. These installations fully comply with all building code and dire safety requirements.

The smoke alarms are powered by the electrical system. A 9-volt battery in each detector is your backup power source if there is an electrical power failure. When the battery is low, you will hear an intermittent beeping or chirping. Replace the battery as necessary; do not simply remove the battery to keep it from chirping, as this will leave your smoke detector non-functional in the event of a power failure.

The push-to-test button accurately tests all smoke alarm functions. Do not use any other test method. Since this is a safety device, the smoke alarm should be tested weekly to ensure proper orientation.

The smoke detector alarm horn is loud in order to alert individuals of a potential danger. However, there may be limiting circumstances where a household member may not hear the alarm (i.e. the hard of hearing, etc.) If you suspect your smoke alarms may not alert a household member, install and maintain specialty smoke alarms.

Typical smoke alarms can only sound their alarms when they detect smoke. Smoke alarms detect combustion particles in the air. They do not sense heat, flame, or gas. This smoke alarm is designed to give audible warning of a developing fire. Smoke may or may not reach the smoke alarm quickly enough to ensure safe escape.

Smoke alarms have limitations. The smoke alarm is not foolproof and is not warranted to protect lives or property from fire. Smoke alarms are not a substitute for fire insurance. Additionally, it is possible for the smoke alarm to fail at any time, for any reason. For this reason, you must test the smoke alarm often and replace the alarm every ten (10) years. Smoke alarms may be triggered by cooking (i.e. by smoke or steam). Familiarize yourself with the proper method to turn-off the smoke alarm when it is clear that there is no danger.

PRATICE FIRE SAFETY! If the smoke alarm sounds and you have not pushed the test button, it is warning of a dangerous situation. Your immediate response is necessary. To prepare for such occurrences, develop family escape plans and consult the local fire department for tips on safety, and discuss them with your household occupants.

MAINTENANCE GUIDELINES

1. The push-to-test button accurately tests all functions. Do not use an open flame to test the smoke alarm as you may ignite and damage the smoke alarm and/or the home.
2. Each smoke alarm unit should be tested often, at least monthly, and upon returning from vacation or when no one has been in the household for an extended period of time.
3. Test all smoke alarms weekly by doing the following:
    a. Observe the green LED. A constant green light indicates the smoke alarm is receiving 120V AC power.
    b. Firmly depress the push-to-test button for several seconds. The smoke alarm will sound a loud beep about four (4) times per second. The alarm may sounds for up to ten (10) seconds after releasing the push-to-test button.
    c. If smoke alarm does not sound, turn off power at main fuse box or circuit breaker and check wiring. Retest the smoke alarm.
4. Replace the backup battery at least once per year. Replace the existing battery with a similar, new, 9-volt battery. Do not use rechargeable batteries. The battery can be replaced as follows:
    a. Turn off power to smoke alarm at main service panel.
    b. Turn the smoke alarm counter-clockwise to detach from mounting plate.
    c. Gently pull down smoke alarm. Be careful not to separate wire connections.
    d. Pull out power plug from back of smoke alarm.
    e. From back of smoke alarm, lift tab to open battery pocket door.
    f. Remove battery from pocket. Disconnect and discard old battery from battery connector.
    g. Connect a new 9-volt battery to connector. The battery will fit only one way. Be sure battery connector is securely attached to battery terminals.
    h. Place battery into battery pocket.

    i. Close battery pocket door. Push down until it snaps into place.
    j. Replace connector plug. Connector will "snap" into place. Gently tug connector to be sure it is attached properly.
    k. Reattach smoke alarm to mounting plate by turning smoke alarm clockwise until it snaps into plate.
    l. Turn on power and test smoke alarm using push-to-test button

5. Using the soft brush attachment to a vacuum cleaner, vacuum all sides and cover of the smoke alarm often and at least monthly to remove dust, dirt or debris. Do not attempt to clean inside the smoke alarm, as this will void the warranty.

HOMEOWNER MAINTENANCE TIPS

The following list of minimum maintenance requirements that should be performed by the Homeowner along with a maintenance schedule. This work should be done either by the Homeowner or by a maintenance person who is experienced and insured. A maintenance person who holds a contractor's license is typically better qualified. Failure to adequately maintain the following areas may eliminate or reduce the Builder's Responsibility if a problem arises.

Bathroom Caulk. The caulk joints in bathrooms need to be inspected and re-caulked (if necessary) every six months. This includes the joint at the bottom of the shower, the joint between the tub and the wall, the joint where the tub or shower pan meets the floor, and vertical inside corners and seats. It is very important that these joints do not pass any water; otherwise dry rot can accumulate regress unseen for years. Joints should be cleaned of old caulk before re-caulking. Any mold or mildew found growing in bathrooms (or other places in the House) should be removed immediately with a mildewcide, available at most hardware stores. The cause of the mold or mildew should be discovered (for example a leaky window or failure to use vent fan while bathing) and the cause subsequently eliminated.

Ceramic Tile Grout. Re-grout or color caulk all cracks after the first year. Once the House frame reaches equilibrium (in less than two years), re-grouting or caulking should not be required. Tile grout should initially be sealed with a silicone based sealer and thereafter every two years.

Chimney Cleaning. The chimney flue should be professionally cleaned every two years if there are more than 50 fires per year or if there are more than 25 fires per year using wax and sawdust logs; subject to any restrictions or requirements of the manufacturer.

Doors. Patio sliding doors should have their tracks (bottom sill) swept and vacuum monthly. The weep holes should also be inspected and cleaned as needed. Dust and dirt build-up in slider door tracks will interfere with the proper operation of the small wheels that the doors slide on. For swing doors, the hinges and latches should be lubricated annually with a dry lubricant specifically made for locks and latches.

Drains

- **Deck.** Deck drains should be flushed with a garden hose and should show evidence of free-flow prior to the start of each rainy season.

- **Yard.** Yard drains should be flushed with a garden hose prior to the start of the rainy season and should show evidence of free flow at the curb or at the sump (if applicable).

- **Sub-drains.** If the House is equipped with a subterranean drainage system around the foundation or through the foundation, the cleanouts (if applicable) of this sub-drain should be flushed prior to the start of the rainy season. There should be evidence of free-flow through the curb or into the sump.

Drywall

- **Cracks.** Minor cracks in drywall usually appear within the first 12 months of occupancy. These cracks typically occur around door frames, cabinets, and window frames and can be easily caulked.

- **Nail Pops.** Nails will sometimes back out of the drywall as the frame of the House dries out. This is not a structural problem, but the nails should be re-driven and the heads should be spackled and painted with touchup paint.

Electrical

- **GFIs.** Ground Fault Interrupters should be tested monthly. When testing, pressing the black TEST button should cause the red or white RESET button to pop out. Push in the RESET button to restore the circuit. If the GFI will not reset, it may be faulty or there may be an open circuit. Contact a qualified, licensed electrical contractor to check the circuit.

- **Closet Ceiling Lights.** Light bulbs in the closets must be covered with a lens or globe as part of the fixture. When changing bulbs in the closet light fixtures, do not exceed the manufacturer's recommended wattage for the build requirement, and do not leave the fixture cover off. Lights left on in closets can generate a significant amount of heat and become a fire hazard.

- **Aluminum Wiring.** While most household wiring is copper, the larger wires (known as cables), are likely to be aluminum. All wires are covered with insulation. Aluminum cables are often used to provide power to air conditioners, heat pumps, electric clothes dryers, and electric ovens. Aluminum is a softer metal than copper. Over time it can deform, or "creep", where it is connected. When aluminum creep occurs, the connection is no longer tight and sparking jumps through the gap. Appliances will consume more power and breakers will trip. It is recommended that the terminal connections of aluminum cables be inspected and tightened if necessary by a qualified, licensed electrical contractor within the first two years after occupancy.

Fencing

- **Wood.** The condition of wood fences should be inspected every spring. Looks for nails that have backed out of boards, fence posts that are leaning and kick boards (at the bottom) that have rotted. All leaning posts should be straightened, all loose boards should be re-nailed and if the kick boards have rotted significantly, they should be replaced.
- **Wrought Iron.** Wrought iron gates and fences should be inspected four times a year to check for rust, particularly at the base of all posts. If rust is discovered, it should be scraped away and the section should be painted with rust-resistant touchup paint.
- **Stucco.** Stucco fencing (patio fencing), should be inspected annually, in the springtime. Cracks on the top of the fence should be caulked and repainted and fence post bases should be inspected or dry rot. All dirt should be removed from the fence post bases.
- **Furnace Filters.** If the House has heating and air conditioning, the furnace filters should be changed at least every six months or at the filter manufacturer's recommendation. If the House has heating only, the furnace filters should be changed prior to the winter season. If the Homeowner lives in an area that has considerable wind driven dust, the above filter change schedule should be doubled.

Garage Doors

- **One piece.** One-piece garage doors (doors that raise and lower one single piece) with automatic openers or garage doors without automatic openers should be lubricated at the hinge points every six months with 30w oil. The keepers (the long threaded rods that run across the top and bottom) should be kept tight to prevent the door from sagging in the middle.

- **Sectional.** Sectional doors (doors that roll up into the garage ceiling on tracks) should have the track rollers lubricated with 30w oil annually.

- **Automatic Opener.** The automatic openers, whether they are chain drive or screw drive, should have the drive mechanism (chain or screw) lubricated with a light grease annually.

- **Bolts.** Garage doors vibrate while opening and closing. Therefore, it is important that an inspection be made every six months for the first year and annually thereafter for bolts that can be wiggled or moved by hand.

- **Weatherstripping.** Check flexibility and contact with floor.

Gutters and Downspouts. Gutters and downspouts should be cleaned and flushed twice annually. The first task is performed just prior to the rainy season, and the second task is performed during the rainy season after the trees have shed their autumn leaves. Prune branches that overhang roofs and gutters..

Insect Control. Insects, particularly termites and carpenter ants, can be harmful to the structure of the House. An annual inspection should be made of the foundation (both on the outside and inside of the crawlspace). Look for brown termite tubes running up the foundation walls and bore holes of the carpenter ants on the exterior of the House. Builders typically do not warrant against any type of insect invasion. Homeowners should pay close attention to pest control maintenance and should not hesitate to call a pest control service if destructive insects are suspected to be present. Firewood should be stored away from the House in a structure or holder that is not in contact with the ground. Do not let vines grow on the House; they will attract insects.

Irrigation Sprinklers. Irrigation sprinklers should be checked annually at the beginning of the growing period (usually March or April) to be sure that the heads are clean and do not spray against the House and that the sprinkler lines have not broken during the winter. Spray patterns should also be checked during the growing season. During the rainy season, irrigation controller times should be changed frequently to avoid overwatering and flooding.

Locks. Once a year, or when they become stiff, apply a dry lubricant as directed into the lock. Use a lubricant specifically designed for locks and avoid use of popular oil synthetic sprays. The latter can form gummy residue on lock parts.

Sink Traps. Depending upon frequency of use, sink traps should be cleaned with a cleanser approved for the type of plumbing pipes under the sink (plastic or metal). For a kitchen sink that receives daily use, a cleaning every 60 days should be sufficient. DO NOT put sink cleaner into a garbage disposal. It may corrode the cutting blade edges.

Solid Surface Countertops. Do not apply countertop surface enhancers or cleansers such as Pledge or 409 to a new solid surface countertop. These products will only attract and hold discoloring items such as coffee, wine, catsup, etc. to the surface. The new nonporous, bacteria-free solid surface countertop will remain in its natural state if it is simply wiped off with a soft sponge or cloth, with an ammonia based product such as glass cleaner, or with a mild soap and water solution. For integral solid surface sinks, use milk abrasive such as "Softscrub" to cut any grease or discoloring buildup that has accumulated on the surface of the sink. Clean off any harsh chemicals such as nail polish remover as soon as possible. Do not cut directly on the solid surface countertop of slide a rough edged objects across the countertop, since these items will create surface scratches in almost any type of countertop. To prevent shocking the surface of any type of sink, do not pour extremely hot grease or water into any sink without simultaneously running cool water. Do not place extremely hot items (such as sheet pans from a 450 degree oven) directly on the countertop or sink.

Trim and Siding. The term "trim" refers to the wooden trim either abutting the stucco or placed on the wooden siding around windows and doors. The trim should be inspected each year prior to the start of the rainy season; and if the trim is pulled away from the House or the caulking has deteriorated, these areas should be re-caulked. If warping or twisting is severe (more than ½ in). the trim should be replaced. Do not caulk the bottom gap of the trim piece over a window or patio door. Also, the siding (exterior wall material such as panels, lap boards, shingles, or other non-stucco, non-brick, or non-stone material such as panels, lap boards, shingles, or other non-stucco, non-brick, or non-stone material) should be inspected for warpage and protruding nails. Inspections should be annual and prior to the start of the rainy season. Warpage should be caulked and painted, and protruding nails should be pulled and replaced with a slightly larger nail. Use hot dipped galvanized box or common nails in exterior applications. Drive the nail head even with the siding; DO NOT drive the nail head into the siding. Driving the nail head into the siding may break the seal and cause the siding to swell and leak during precipitation. Touch up all work with caulk and paint.

Vents. This includes kitchen hood filters and bathroom laundry fans. The hood filters should be removed and washed with a grease removing cleanser at least 4 times a year (depending upon use). Bathroom and laundry fans should be vacuumed with a hose vacuum and crevice tool at least once a year. Clothes dryer vents must be kept open lint free. Accumulation of lint will significantly reduce the efficiency of the dryer and, under some circumstances, become a source of fire in the duct. Depending upon the degree of use, and the length of the dryer duct, the dryer vent ducts should be cleaned every two to five years.

Water Heater. To prolong the life of the water heater, accumulated sediment should be removed from the heater tank once a year. This task can be performed by attaching a thick wall garden hose to the drain spigot at the bottom of the tank and draining out no more than two gallons. **Since the water being drained is very hot, be very careful that the hot water does not come into contact with persons, animals, plants, or any material that could be damaged by scalding water (120 degrees F to 160 degrees F).**

Windows (includes Patio doors)

- **Seals.** Inspect for broken or breached window seals in dual pane windows at least annually. Windows with broken or breached seals are easily identified by having a moist, foggy, or filmy condition between the two panes of glass. When this condition exists, the insulating value of the window is greatly diminished. The only repair is to replace the window.

- **Weep Holes.** The weep holes at the bottom of windows and patio doors serve a purpose: to allow water to drain out from the track during rainstorms. Weep holes should be inspected at least annually to make sure that no debris has plugged the holes and that rainwater will drain freely from them.

- **Tracks.** The tracks of windows and patio doors should be swept and vacuumed frequently to prevent dust and debris buildup. Clean window and door tracks, allowing the sliding vent to move more freely, so that the drainage through the weep holes will not be impaired by any wet debris. In open areas where there is ongoing construction or agricultural operations that generate dust, track cleaning should be done weekly.

BIBLIOGRAPHY AND REFERENCES

American Concrete Institute. (2011). *ACI 318-Building Code Requirements for Structural Concrete.* Farmington Hills, MI.

American Concrete Institute. (2011). *ACI 530- Building Code Requirements for Masonry Structures.* Farmington Hills, MI.

American Forest and Paper Association. (2011) *Wood Frame Construction Manual for One- and Two-Family Dwellings (WFCM).* Leesburg, VA.

American Iron and Steel Institute. (2007). *Standard for Cold-Formed Steel Framing—Prescriptive Method for One - and Two-Family Dwellings (AISI S230).* Washington D.C.

American Society of Heating, Refrigerating and Air-Conditioning Engineers. (2006-2009). *ASHRAE Handbook: Fundamentals.* Atlanta, GA.

Ballast, D. (1994). *Handbook of Construction Tolerances.* McGraw Hill.

Building Industry Association of San Diego County. (1993). *Top 25 Construction Problems and Their Resolution.* Construction Quality Task Force.

California Building Industry Association. (2005). *SB 800, The Homebuilder "FIX IT" Construction Dispute Resolution Law.* Sacramento, CA.

California, State of, Department of Real Estate. (1996). *Operating Cost Manual for Homeowner Association.* Sacramento, CA.

California, State of, Contractor's State License Board. (1982). *Workmanship Guidelines.* Sacramento, CA.

Concrete Committee of San Diego County. (2001). *Concrete Performance Standards and Maintenance guidelines.* San Diego, CA.

Gypsum Association. (2012). *Fire Resistance Design Manual.* Hyattsville, MD.

Hansen, D. & Kardon, R. (2011). *Code Check – Building.* Taunton Press. Newtown, CT.

Hansen, D. & Kardon, R. (2010). *Code Check – Electrical.* Taunton Press. Newtown, CT.

Hansen, D. & Kardon, R. (2011). *Code Check – Plumbing &Mechanical.* Taunton Press. Newtown, CT.

International Code Council. (2007). *California Building Code.* Whittier, CA.

International Code Council. (2007). *California Electrical Code.* Whittier, CA.

International Code Council. (2007). *California Mechanical Code.* Whittier, CA.

International Code Council. (2007). *California Plumbing Code.* Whittier, CA.

International Code Council. (2006-2009). *International Residential Code for One and Two Family Dwellings.* Washington D.C.

International Association of Plumbing & Mechanical Officials. (2009). *Uniform Mechanical Code.* Ontario, CA.

International Association of Plumbing & Mechanical Officials. (2009). *Uniform Plumbing Code.* Ontario, CA.

Journal of Light Construction. (1997). *Troubleshooting Guide to Residential Construction*, Builderburg Group.

NAHM Research Center, Inc. (2001). *Mold in Residential Buildings.* Washington D.C.

National Association of State Contracting Licensing Agencies. (2009). *NASCLA Residential Construction Standards.* Phoenix, AZ.

National Fire Protection Association. (2011). *National Electrical Code.*

National Roofing Contractor's Association. (2007-1009). *NCRA Roofing and Waterproofing Manual.* Vols 1, 2, & 3. Rosemont, IL.

National Wood Flooring Association. (2000). *Problems, Causes and Cures.* Ellisville, MO.

NAHB Home Builder Press. (2005). *Residential Construction Performance Guidelines.* Washington D.C.

New Jersey, State of, Division of Codes and Standards. (2005). *Homeowners booklet,* New Home Warranty Program. NJ.

Reynolds, D. (1998). *Residential & Light Commercial Construction Standards.* R.S. Means, Inc. Kingston, MA.

Sacks, A. (1994). *Residential Water Problems.* NAHM Home Builder Press. Washington, DC.

Structural Building Component Association & Truss Plate Institute. (2006-2013). *Guide to Good Practice for Handling, Installing, Restraining & Bracing of Metal Plate Connected Wood Trusses.*

Tenebaum, D. (1996). *The Complete Idiot's Guide to Trouble Free Home Repair.* Alpha Books. NY.

Truss Plate Institute. (2008). *National Design Standard for Metal Plate Connected Wood Truss Construction.* Alexandria, VA.

ABOUT THE AUTHOR

Ryan Brautovich is an Army veteran with more than 20 years of home construction, home remodeling and building experience who has consulted for Fortune 500 home builders as well as the Top 100 privately held home building companies. He is a custom home builder in California and a California licensed general contractor. Ryan is International Code Council Certified, an International and California Building Inspector as well as an International and California Plumbing Inspector. He is a graduate of Auburn University with degrees in both Accounting and Business Management. He has consulted for the City of Lancaster (CA) Building & Safety Department, K. Hovnanian Homes, Beezer Homes, Pardee Homes, KB Homes, Standard Pacific Homes, American Premiere Homes, Richmond American Homes, DR Horton, and Frontier Homes – just to name a few.

Ryan founded the Construction H.E.L.P. Foundation, a national nonprofit organization, dedicated to advocating for and meeting the needs of individuals who have suffered at the hands of unscrupulous contractors and sub-contractors who simply took advantage of the helpless homeowner in order to make a quick buck – and either didn't finish the project, overcharged or simply took money and didn't perform the work as promised. Over the years, the number of phone calls Ryan received increased dramatically from frustrated and angry homeowners who were desperately seeking help after being ripped off by other contractors. As a result, he founded the Construction H.E.L.P. Foundation, and it's educational assistance program – Home Construction Audit – to provide assistance and education to homeowners. As the President of the Construction H.E.L.P. Foundation, Ryan has made it the organization's daily mission to return ethics to the home building and home remodeling profession and provide homeowners with the expert help and crucial knowledge they need so that they will never be taken advantage of again.

www.ingramcontent.com/pod-product-compliance
Lightning Source LLC
Chambersburg PA
CBHW021852300426
44115CB00005B/134